*Social
Behaviour and
Network
Therapy for
Alcohol
Problems*

**ALEX COPELLO,
JIM ORFORD,
RAY HODGSON AND
GILLIAN TOBER**

Routledge
Taylor & Francis Group

LONDON AND NEW YORK

First published 2009 by Routledge
27 Church Road, Hove, East Sussex BN3 2FA

Simultaneously published in the USA and Canada
by Routledge
270 Madison Avenue, New York, NY 10016

Routledge is an imprint of the Taylor & Francis Group, an Informa business

© 2009 Alex Copello, Jim Orford, Ray Hodgson and Gillian Tober

Typeset in Stone Serif by Garfield Morgan, Swansea, West Glamorgan
Printed and bound in Great Britain by TJ International, Padstow, Cornwall
Cover design by Andy Ward

British Library Cataloguing in Publication Data
A catalogue record for this book is available from the British Library

Library of Congress Cataloging-in-Publication Data
Social behaviour and network therapy for alcohol problems / Alex
Copello . . . [et al.].
      p. cm.
   ISBN 978-1-58391-803-6 (pbk. only)
   1. Alcoholism counseling. 2. Alcoholism–Treatment. 3. Alcoholics–
Family relationships. 4. Alcoholics–Social networks. I. Copello, Alex,
1957–
   HV5275.S63 2009
   616.86'106–dc22
                                                          2009005042

ISBN: 978-1-58391-803-6 (pbk only)

Social Behaviour and Network Therapy for Alcohol Problems

Alex Copello is Professor of Addiction Research at the University of Birmingham and Consultant Clinical Psychologist at Birmingham and Solihull Mental Health Foundation Trust.

Jim Orford is Emeritus Professor of Clinical and Community Psychology at the University of Birmingham.

Ray Hodgson is Director of the Alcohol Education and Research Council.

Gillian Tober is Honorary Consultant in Addiction Psychology, Head of Training and Clinical Services Manager at the Leeds Addiction Unit.

Social Behaviour and Network Therapy for Alcohol Problems serves as a manual for clinicians working with people with alcohol problems. The manual is based on previous research in addiction treatment, including family and social network interventions, as well the authors' own work developing and evaluating Social Behaviour and Network Therapy (SBNT) for example in the United Kingdom Alcohol Treatment Trial (UKATT).

Containing a range of ideas the book is guided by a key principle: the development of social support for a positive change in drinking behaviour.

Divided into three parts topics include:

⦿ an introduction to the evidence base underpinning SBNT
⦿ core components of the treatment
⦿ common questions asked about the intervention.

Featuring a series of practical handouts, this book will be essential reading for clinicians, counsellors, nurses, psychologists and all those involved in the treatment of alcohol misuse and dependence.

This manual was shaped by our work and experience with the United Kingdom Alcohol Treatment Trial (UKATT) and our invaluable work with UKATT colleagues.

Contents

Figures and tables

Figures

Tables

About the authors

Alex Copello arrived in the UK from Argentina in 1977. He is a Consultant Clinical Psychologist and formerly clinical director of the Birmingham and Solihull National Health Service (NHS) Foundation Trust substance misuse services, the Director for the Trust Applied Addiction Research and Development Programme and Professor of Addiction Research at the School of Psychology, University of Birmingham. His career has combined clinical and academic work in the addiction field. His research and clinical interests include the study of the impact of addiction upon families as well as the development and evaluation of family and social network based interventions. He publishes regularly in a number of scientific journals. He has been a member of the executive council of the Society for the Study of Addiction and is currently the chair of the New Directions in the Study of Alcohol Group in the UK.

Jim Orford has researched and written about alcohol and other potentially addictive behaviours throughout his career, and now heads the Alcohol, Drugs, Gambling and Addiction Research Group in the School of Psychology at the University of Birmingham, where he is Emeritus Professor of Clinical and Community Psychology. Among his best known works is *Excessive Appetites: A Psychological View of Addictions* (2nd edition, Wiley, 2001). His latest book is *Community Psychology: Challenges, Controversies and Emerging Consensus* (Wiley, 2008).

Ray Hodgson was Director of the Cardiff Alcohol Research Unit within the University of Wales College of Medicine until 2003. He started his career in the field of addiction at the Addiction Research Unit in the Institute of Psychiatry. He then directed the Cardiff Clinical Psychology service within the NHS. He has been a World Health Organization adviser on alcohol and drugs, deputy editor of *Addiction*, Editor of the *Journal of Mental Health* and the *British Journal of Clinical Psychology* and President of the Society for the Study of Addiction. He has published on a wide range of issues in the addiction field including psychological treatments, health promotion, screening and dependence.

Gillian Tober is Honorary Consultant in Addiction Psychology and Head of Training at the Leeds Addiction Unit, and Honorary Senior Lecturer at the University of Leeds. She practises and supervises evidence based psycho-social treatment including Social Behaviour and Network Therapy in a large clinical service. She was the Principal Investigator for the National Training Centre in the United Kingdom Alcohol Treatment Trial, responsible for training, supervising and monitoring UKATT therapists. Her research is in the measurement of the process of treatment delivery, the effectiveness of addiction treatment and the nature and measurement of substance dependence. She is President of the Society for the Study of Addiction.

Preface

The conventional wisdom regarding the treatment of alcohol and other forms of substance misuse is that there are only two parties involved. One is the substance misusing individual himself or herself, who is responsible for initiating and maintaining change. The other is the professional therapist, and the team or organisation within which the therapist works, who are responsible for delivering the therapeutic intervention. It is largely a private matter between the individual and the therapeutic person or system. Sometimes a mutual-help organisation, like Alcoholics Anonymous (AA), takes the place of the treatment unit, and an AA sponsor may play a special role. But in all cases it is the individual who is thinking about changing substance use who is the exclusive focus. Other people in that person's natural environment, such as family members or friends, are not normally considered, and if they are, their role is peripheral to the main action. Their marginal position in the treatment enterprise is illustrated by the term 'third parties', which is a term by which they are sometimes known. The whole business of treatment is very individualistic.

There is another way of approaching the treatment of substance misuse that recognises the central role that can be played by others who are affected by and concerned about the focal client's excessive alcohol or other drug use. A cautious estimate of the number of adults who are seriously affected by the excessive substance use of a close relative is three-quarters of a million in Britain, 7–8 million in Europe as a whole, and 80 million world-wide. Some experts would double or even triple those figures to produce an estimate of the number of concerned and affected adults. Those estimates leave out of account the millions of children whose lives are adversely affected in some way as a result of living in a household where a parent has an alcohol or other substance misuse problem. It also fails to count the millions of close friends, work colleagues and others who are concerned about someone with such a problem. Social Behaviour and Network Therapy (SBNT), the subject of this manual, brings concerned and affected adult family members and friends into the centre of the picture. In the language of SBNT they are 'network members'. They become clients of the treatment enterprise themselves. Since the person they are concerned about is therefore not the only client, SBNT refers to that person as the 'focal client'.

SBNT creates new positions for everyone concerned. Focal clients, rather than being viewed as the ones who must take all the responsibility for change, are now seen as people who need to draw on the support from family members and friends that is available to them in their social networks. Family and friends (the network members), rather than being kept on the margins, or even, as has sometimes been the case, being blamed for contributing to the problem, are now cast in the role of supporters of change. They are seen as central players and their roles are positive ones. While this is positive, it is also challenging. The role of significant supporter of a focal client's efforts to change will be unfamiliar to many family members and friends. The role may be unwelcome to some and too demanding for others. Like many aspects of SBNT these new roles may not be at all what focal clients and their family members and friends expect, more familiar as they are likely to be with an individualised model of health and social care.

This is a new way of working in the treatment of alcohol problems and it also represents a challenge to those professionals – which means nearly all of us – who have been trained in the more conventional style that emphasises one-to-one therapist-to-client counselling or psychotherapy. Indeed the very word 'therapist' becomes problematic under the new set of assumptions associated with SBNT. Might 'network facilitator' or 'group leader' be more appropriate? Those who come to practise SBNT may find their own answers to that question. In any case SBNT is comparatively new and may change and develop in ways that cannot be foreseen. Although this manual provides the basic grounding in SBNT, we would not want it to become a fixed set of techniques. We would prefer to see it as a concept that will lead to new and evolving forms of practice.

SBNT was first developed for a large multi-centre alcohol problems treatment trial in the UK (the United Kingdom Alcohol Treatment Trial or UKATT) but we believe it has application well beyond drinking problems. Since the initial trial it has been used to good effect in the treatment of problems related to the misuse of drugs other than alcohol. We think it would be equally applicable in the treatment of other addiction or dependence problems including problem gambling. Its relevance may be wider still. Recent years have seen growing awareness of, and knowledge about, the stresses experienced and concerns expressed by family members and friends of people experiencing any one of a broad range of physical, psychological and social difficulties. Although addiction may constitute a unique and particularly troubling set of circumstances for network members, there are many features in common with other forms of difficulty. The support that family and friends can provide for someone struggling with an addiction problem is similar in many ways to the support that parents provide for a child with a chronic illness or an adolescent showing disruptive behaviour disorder. There are similarities, too, with the support that family members or other carers provide for older people with dementia, or for those with chronic physical or mental illness, or even – to cite an example of a condition that has been well described in the literature – with the support that wives give to husbands who return from active military service suffering from combat stress reaction. These are all examples of circumstances in which an individualised model of distress and treatment is slowly giving way to one that recognises the central role that family members and friends have to play in positively supporting the person who is primarily affected. SBNT is part of that growing movement.

SBNT is comparatively new. We believe it is full of promise but many questions remain. One thing is certain however. Social influence is a very important factor in the development, maintenance and recovery from addictions and other physical and mental health problems including for example depression and schizophrenia. Current research suggests that the power of social influence or social support has to be incorporated into treatment. This manual attempts to facilitate this ambitious task.

Acknowledgements

In keeping with the theme of the manual, there is a large network of people that we would like to acknowledge for their contribution to the development of Social Behaviour and Network Therapy. Alison Moore and Janet Ellis were instrumental in the early piloting and feasibility work. We would like to thank our other collaborators in the United Kingdom Alcohol Treatment Trial, Duncan Raistrick, Nick Heather, Ian Russell and Christine Godfrey as well as Gary Slegg, the trial coordinator, for their valuable help in developing this approach and their helpful comments along the way. We are also grateful to other members of the UKATT research team including Cecily Kerr, Tina Alwyn, Gill Thistlethwaite, Kate Carlyle, Linda Handsworth, Rachel Black, Bev John, Melanie Smith and Rob Kenyon.

Alan Atkinson and Clive Barrett were both supervisors for Social Behaviour and Network Therapy in the UKATT and made a significant contribution in the thinking and development of SBNT. Later, Emmie Williamson, Sheila Wilton and Ed Day helped to adapt SBNT to work with drug users and helped with the development of handout materials and ways of presenting the contents in a more clear style. We are also grateful to Sarah Galvani for helping us in thinking about issues of violence and potential abuse.

Our grateful thanks go to Pat Evans in Birmingham UK, who prepared draft and final versions of the manuscript for this manual and Gail Crossley for help with the production of some materials. We are also grateful to Sue Copello for numerous comments on drafts of the manual.

We would like to acknowledge the support of the Medical Research Council, which funded the UKATT where SBNT was evaluated.

Some materials have been reproduced from Yates' work with permission from Wiley. The contents of Table 6 have been adapted with permission from Taylor and Francis and the materials included in Table 7 are reproduced with permission from Wiley.

Our greatest thanks go to all the people with alcohol problems and their concerned and affected network members who received SBNT and the numerous therapists that have delivered this treatment over the last few years. We hope that the ideas contained in this manual will continue to stimulate thinking and provide help and support to those affected by these highly prevalent and challenging problems.

Online resources

The appendices of this book contain worksheets that can be downloaded free of charge to purchasers of the print version. Please visit the website www.routledgementalhealth.com/social-behaviour-network-therapy to find out more about this facility.

Manual format

This manual has been written for clinicians working with people with alcohol problems. This may include counsellors, nurses, psychologists, alcohol workers, generic workers and some medical practitioners. The contents are based on previous research in addiction treatment including family and social network interventions as well as our own work developing and evaluating this approach. The manual has been used to train clinicians including those delivering Social Behaviour and Network Therapy in the UK Alcohol Treatment Trial where it was found to be as effective and as cost-effective as Motivational Enhancement Therapy.

The manual is a practical tool and contains a range of ideas guided by a key principle: the development of 'social support for a positive change in drinking behaviour'. The main body of the manual is divided into three parts.

Part I starts with an introduction to the evidence base underpinning SBNT followed by a description of the treatment philosophy, the necessary therapist skills as well as the content and the structure of the intervention. An important aspect of SBNT is the philosophy based on the notion that 'social network support for change' is an essential ingredient for successful treatment of alcohol problems. All components and strategies described are therefore guided by this key principle.

Part II covers the core components of the treatment that all clients receiving SBNT should be exposed to. The early part of SBNT involves communicating the rationale for a social approach, identifying each client's social network and agreeing a treatment goal. This work is common to all cases. We have used the idea of core and elective material that has also been used in other treatment manuals. This allows flexibility so that clinicians can deliver the core components but also select additional components that might be particularly suitable for an individual case. We call them topics instead of sessions. The reason for this is that we describe the rationale and principles for each topic before we provide a range of practical suggestions as to how the topic can be used. Which specific strategy is used as part of a topic (say for example communication) will depend upon the needs of each particular case. This will become clearer as you become more familiar with the manual content.

The core topics include communication, coping with alcohol problems, enhancing social support and relapse management.

Part III includes all the elective topics. These can be used flexibly and chosen for relevance to each individual case. Elective topics include basic information about alcohol, increasing pleasant and joint activities, employment, active development of positive support for those who are isolated and minimising support for problematic drinking. Training and supervision issues are discussed in Part III and we have also included a section outlining common questions that have been asked about the intervention.

Finally we have a series of prompt sheets that can serve as a resource for those receiving SBNT or memory aids for the therapists.

Throughout the manual, a number of case examples are used to illustrate the different strategies and aspects of the treatment. Case material is based on our own clinical work, although names and details have been changed to preserve anonymity. It is essential that all the components in Part I are fully understood before embarking on studying the detail of the treatment.

Background, evidence base, treatment content and format

Theoretical and research basis for Social Behaviour and Network Therapy

BACKGROUND

Social Behaviour and Network Therapy (SBNT) is derived from a number of different social and family approaches to the treatment of alcohol problems and aims to work with a positive part of the client's social network to provide a coherent set of coping strategies for both the person with the drinking problem and network members such as family, friends and work colleagues. These coping strategies can be used both within the treatment period and following treatment completion. Research evidence has informed the development of SBNT and some of this evidence is discussed. The following section is not meant to include a comprehensive review of the research literature in this area. Instead, our aim is to highlight some of the key evidence that has informed the development of SBNT. For a more detailed consideration of some of the areas discussed, the reader is referred to the research papers and reviews quoted.

Early overviews of the alcohol treatment literature (e.g. Holder et al. 1991; Finney and Monahan 1996) suggested that the social components of treatment for alcohol problems (e.g. Community Reinforcement, Social Skills Training, Behavioural Marital Therapy) were among those with the greatest evidence of positive treatment outcome when compared with other types of treatment. More recent reviews have confirmed this conclusion. After a comprehensive and systematic review of the alcohol treatment literature, Miller and Wilbourne (2002: 276) concluded that 'Attention to the person's social context and support system is prominent among several of the most supported approaches'. In 2007 a systematic review of the clinical and cost-effectiveness of interventions involving families and friends in alcohol misuse and dependence analysed the results of thirty-four randomised controlled trials (Meads et al. 2007). Results suggested that compared with other interventions, therapies involving families and friends led to higher percentage of abstinent days, improved family functioning and were more effective at encouraging treatment entry rates for the problem drinker.

Research has supported the notion that social networks can be highly influential in terms of helping people with drinking problems to initiate treatment (e.g. Barber and Crisp 1995; Meyers and Smith 1995; Meyers et al. 1996; Miller et al. 1999), in affecting the course and outcome of interventions (e.g. McCrady et al. 1986, 1990; Stout et al. 1987, 1990; Stanton and Shadish 1997) and influencing the likelihood of relapse and long-term maintenance of change (e.g. Marlatt and Gordon 1985; O'Farrell et al. 1993; McCrady et al. 1999). In her paper entitled 'To have but one true friend', Barbara McCrady (2004) explores the role that social networks play in the recognition and resolution of drinking problems. Important factors discussed by McCrady include the structure of social networks, the influence of social networks on the person with the drinking problem in terms of problem recognition and help-seeking, the influences on treatment outcome and the involvement of the networks both during treatment and after care. McCrady (2004) discusses the evidence for the positive and negative impacts that social networks can have. The author goes on to suggest that social networks of people with alcohol problems can both support and impede successful recognition and change and suggests that alcohol treatment needs to pay close attention to the role of social networks in terms of problem recognition; assisting treatment entry and involvement and support both during and after treatment periods.

Findings from the Project MATCH Research Group (1997), the largest study of treatment for alcohol problems, provide further evidence of the central role that social factors can play in drinking behaviour. Patients whose social network was supportive of their drinking had poorer outcomes in all treatment conditions. Mohr et al. (2001) conducted further analyses of the MATCH data specifically focused on friends within problem drinkers' networks. The study found that those clients who reduced the proportion of drinking friends in their social networks drank less at follow-up when compared with clients who continued to have a high proportion of drinking friends. Also, the study reported that an increase in the number of non-drinking friends at follow-up was associated with a reduced number of drinks per drinking day. In addition, Longabaugh et al. (1993) had previously shown that poorer outcomes for drinking were associated with networks that were not supportive of abstinence in clients pursuing this goal. It therefore becomes important to attempt to both enhance and increase network support for the client's chosen drinking goal as well as to decrease any support for the continuation of problem drinking.

THE IMPACT OF AN ALCOHOL PROBLEM ON SOCIAL NETWORKS

Previous research into the effects of drinking on close family (Orford et al. 1975, 2005; Yates 1988) or colleagues at work (Molloy 1989) illustrates the importance of a clear and shared understanding of the problem by all those affected. This research suggests that when individuals begin to drink heavily, people around them including family and friends do not always have sufficient knowledge to decide whether or not their drinking is excessive, and if they do know it is excessive, they often do not know what to do about it or how to respond. A common scenario is that members of the network either ignore the problem or talk to people other than the person experiencing the drinking problem about the situation. On occasions, their actions may unwittingly compound the drinking problem. The message that the network gives to the person with a drinking problem will affect the situation (Leventhal et al. 1980; Hasin 1994). SBNT addresses the problem of confusion in the network of the person with a drinking problem by helping both the latter and the network to come to a decision about whether or not a drinking problem exists. Providing information about drinking alcohol and its effects can be helpful in this process. The therapist also seeks to utilise the concerned network member's desire to help and attempts to unify the message that the network gives to the person with the drinking problem.

In his book *Fragmented Intimacy* Peter Adams (2008) offers an insightful view of addiction problems within a social context. Discussing the initiation of treatment, Adams highlights the dangers of services that are normally focused on the individual with the addiction problem, adding further fragmentation into the social system. Family members, reassured by the fact that their loved one is in contact with expert help, may withdraw in order to allow the services to deliver their expert interventions. However, there is a danger that when progress is slow or problematic, family members and those close to the person with the addiction problem, who are mostly excluded from the process, become more confused and continue to distance themselves from their loved one. The social orientation of SBNT attempts to minimise this risk by focusing on and engaging with the social network.

FAMILY AND NETWORK TREATMENTS

There has been a comparatively recent change of emphasis in some of the treatments for alcohol problems involving the widening of the focus of attention to consider the potential value of including concerned friends and family members in treatment and this has been reflected in the higher number of published studies in this area. Two reviews (Copello et al. 2005, 2006a) proposed three types of interventions that involve family members and others concerned and affected by the alcohol or drug use of someone else:

- interventions that aim to achieve engagement of the substance user through working with the affected social network (e.g. Pressures to Change, Community Reinforcement and Family Training)
- interventions that involve both the users and family and friends jointly in treatment (e.g. Behavioural Couples Therapy, Network Therapy, Social Behaviour and Network Therapy)
- interventions that focus on the needs of affected family members in their own right (e.g. Behavioural Exchange Systems; Training Interventions for partners of problem drinkers, the five-step intervention for affected family members).

Evaluations carried out to date suggest that a number of the family and network methods show promise, particularly those focused on problems related to alcohol misuse that have been the focus of most research in this area.

Promoting help seeking and engagement

As stated, some of the approaches have concentrated on working with the spouse and the family in the absence of the person with a drinking problem and some aspects of these approaches have been included in SBNT. An example of these types of intervention is the 'pressures to change' approach that uses the family to influence the person with a drinking problem. It starts by engaging the concerned family member in treatment and working with him/her by increasing the understanding of the problem through education, discussing setting up activities incompatible with drinking, exploring the partner's response to drinking and finally preparing the family member to confront the person with the problem and request that he/she approaches services to obtain help with the drinking problem. In essence, this approach aims to create changes in the behaviour of those concerned and affected by the person with a drinking problem with the hope that the latter will be induced into treatment. In a controlled study (Barber and Crisp 1995) it was found that more people with drinking problems engaged in treatment services after their relatives were treated with the 'pressures to change' approach as compared with those who received no treatment. Unilateral family therapy is another approach that focuses on working with family members in the absence of the person with the drinking problem and has been shown to produce decreases in drinking in the untreated spouse (Thomas and Ager 1993).

Yates' (1988) work constitutes a further example of an approach that actively initiates contacts with anyone who may be affected by the drinking and can potentially benefit the client in his/her efforts to change. Given that in a number of cases, people in the network will have partial information and perhaps not have combined forces to understand and respond effectively to the problem, professionals may need to be active in engaging potentially helpful parts of the social network in treatment and this is illustrated by the work of Yates. The following two cases reported by Yates (1988) illustrate some powerful ways of working by focusing beyond the individual client:

Case 1

This problem drinker's case was brought forward by her mother, who was worried that her daughter's drinking could result in the break-up of her marriage and separation from her three children. This drinker was often drunk and bad tempered and family entreaties to reduce her drinking had met with little success. Her husband was often away from home on long-term contracts. At the second appointment we arranged to see the problem drinker and her eldest daughter. Our success in getting the drinker in front of us was a big step forward. She had never sought help before and had admitted the problem within the family only very recently. We saw her over four visits, at which she reported complete success in controlling her drinking. We next received a call from the drinker's mother, who gave us a different picture of events. The next appointment was made with the drinker and her husband. This was a long and difficult session. Our client agreed to make a final attempt to save her marriage by confronting her drinking problem and the husband agreed to support her if she was serious, but would seek separation if another lapse occurred. She agreed to attend group sessions for women problem drinkers and at follow-up reported that her marriage was much happier and the drinking under control. This was confirmed by her mother.

Case 2

This case began as a visit from the parents of a 28-year-old male problem drinker. He had been drinking heavily for at least five years and had recently been admitted to a local general hospital for pancreatitis. His marriage was only three months old and was already being threatened by his drinking. Both his parents and wife had been resourceful in strategies to reduce the drinking before consulting us. They had made appeals to him to stop, tried to engage him in other activities, controlled the money he had available and drunk with him in an effort to keep his consumption down. We were able to make telephone contact with his wife and she gave us a similar story to that of his parents. Surprisingly, his hospital admission for pancreatitis had not resulted in a referral to an alcohol counselling agency – he had only been cautioned about his drinking. We were finally successful, after more calls, in getting him to come to see us and agreed for his admission to the Alcohol Treatment Unit as an outpatient. At follow-up he was still seeing a doctor from the Unit for his drinking problem. His mother reported that his drinking had greatly improved, an assessment upheld by the hospital registrar.

(Reproduced with permission from *British Journal of Addiction*, Wiley)

These two examples illustrate clearly the powerful role of social networks in affecting change as well as the active role that therapists had to adopt in order to engage both concerned others and focal drinkers in the treatment process.

Working jointly with concerned and affected others and the person with the drinking problem

An emphasis on working with family members in order, ultimately, to help the problem drinking individual is used by Meyers and colleagues (Meyers and Smith 1995; Meyers et al. 1996) in the community reinforcement approach (CRA). The latter is a development and refinement of the original community reinforcement treatment reported by Azrin and colleagues (Hunt and Azrin 1973; Azrin 1976; Azrin et al. 1982). The essential idea within this treatment was that of restructuring social, family and vocational aspects of everyday living of those with drinking problems so that sobriety was selectively encouraged while drinking was discouraged. Early evaluations of the community reinforcement approach showed that better outcomes could be achieved with this treatment when compared with a control condition. There have been a number of studies with alcohol and other drug problems providing strong empirical evidence for the CRA approach (e.g. Higgins et al. 1993; Abbott et al. 1998; Gruber et al. 2000). A review by Smith et al. (2001) confirmed the positive outcomes of CRA across a range of clients and problem substances.

Other approaches aim to engage family members in the treatment process in order to enhance positive outcomes. Some of these treatments have focused on improving relationships, decreasing behaviours that facilitate drinking as well as drinking control strategies, increasing marital stability and introducing other strategies designed to create a positive basis for change in the drinker's behaviour. These treatments have resulted in better outcomes than approaches that do not involve the drinker's family (O'Farrell et al. 1985) and in the long term show an increase in the number of days spent abstinent compared with minimal spouse involvement conditions (McCrady et al. 1986; Stout et al. 1987). A good example of an intervention that involves problem drinkers and their partners is behavioural marital and couples therapy. The latter intervention has been the subject of a programme of well-designed research studies. Through a systematic programme, the treatment aims to assess and increase positive behavioural interactions between the substance user and partner and improve communication skills. Evaluations of this approach have shown reductions in the substance misuse behaviour but also improvements in martial adjustment and levels of domestic violence (O'Farrell et al. 1992; O'Farrell and Murphy 1995; Kelley and Fals-Stewart 2002; Walitzer and Dermen 2004).

Drawing on the work discussed so far, in SBNT the powerful influence of concerned others is used to support the person with the drinking problem and also to attempt to re-engage the person in treatment should he/she temporarily lose contact with the service during the treatment period. Further discussion in relation to this area is provided in later sections within the manual.

Support for those affected in their own right

A different type of approach of theoretical relevance is focused on the needs of those affected by the drinking, mainly family members, as people who are under stress and at risk of developing health problems in their own right (e.g. Copello et al. 2000a, 2000b; Howells and Orford 2006). The latter approaches emphasise discussing with family members different ways of coping. Both the approach used by Howells and Orford (2006) and that reported by Copello and colleagues have been shown to change family members' coping responses resulting in improvements in health and well-being. Howells and Orford (2006) showed how several reported ways of coping by wives changed over a period of six months following the start of individual intervention. Howells and Orford concluded that significant reductions in self-sacrificing behaviour could be made relatively quickly by wives once they had discussed ways of coping with a counsellor and had explored options available to them. Changes in self-sacrificing coping were also associated with a general improvement in health for the wives as measured by the Symptom Rating Test (Kellner and Sheffield 1973). Copello and colleagues showed how a brief five-step intervention delivered to family members in primary care, led to similar results in terms of changed coping and symptom reduction for family members. Both approaches were informed by the stress-strain-coping-support model of addiction and the family developed by Orford and colleagues (Orford et al. 1992; Orford 1994, 1998; Orford et al. 1998a, 1998b, 1998c) and some of the central ideas from this approach are included within the core topics of SBNT both to be used when attempting to work with those close to the problem drinker or when trying to understand their responses to the drinking behaviour.

Involving wider social networks

Some authors have argued that the drinker's larger social network should be included in treatment (e.g. Beattie et al. 1993). One of the few social interventions that directly engages the wider social networks in the treatment process is network therapy (Galanter 1993a). Network therapy is an approach to the treatment of alcohol and drug problems that emphasises the involvement of people from a number of different areas of the identified drinker's life, for example friends and work colleagues. Selected family members and friends are enlisted in treatment to provide ongoing support and promote both attitude and behaviour change. The networks used can be of any size and everyone who is willing to attend would attend the treatment sessions.

The role of the network is to work together as a team and hence the treatment defines network members as part of the therapist's team not subjects of treatment. Abstinence is emphasised as a goal of treatment and cohesiveness is stressed, the challenge of changing maladaptive attitudes and cognitions is undertaken and the influential force of the network upon the drinker's behaviour is utilised. In an evaluation of network therapy (Galanter 1993b) the outcome for sixty patients was described. It was found that 92 per cent of the sample was treated with at least one other network member and the average size of network for this group was 2.3 members. Of the fifty-five clients treated with a network, 36 per cent had a member of their family of origin participating, 27 per cent had a network whose only member was their partner, 7 per cent had networks consisting of only peers. Overall, 77 per cent of the total group (n=60) experienced major or full improvement. Major improvement was defined as a marked decline in substance use to non-problem levels along with at least some improvement in psychological and/or social state and full improvement was defined as the maintenance of abstinence for at least six months and an appreciable enhancement in social and/or psychological adjustment. These findings are promising although further evaluation including a control group would be useful.

Some elements of Network Therapy have been included in SBNT, in particular the engagement of wider social networks in treatment and the rules for selection of supportive network members.

A more recent study conducted by Litt et al. (2007) aimed to influence through the delivery of a network support intervention the composition of the networks of people with alcohol problems entering treatment. The study compared Network Support, Network Support in addition to Contingency Management and Case Management. Two hundred and ten outpatients were randomly assigned to receive one of the treatment conditions. The findings showed that the network support intervention increased support for abstinence in the networks as well as leading to increased involvement in Alcoholic Anonymous. They concluded that social networks of people with alcohol problems can be changed through intervention and that increases in support for abstinence improve treatment outcomes.

SBNT EARLY FEASIBILITY WORK

Early in the development of SBNT we conducted a feasibility evaluation (Ellis 1998) of a manual-based treatment termed Network Support Therapy (Copello et al. 1997) within a National Health Service treatment setting in the UK. Network Support Therapy was a precursor to SBNT that included the same key areas used in treatment and shared with SBNT the central philosophy of the enhancement of social network positive support for change. One main difference was the fact that no specific provision was made to work with those clients who were isolated or who had difficult relationships with potential network members. As part of this study, seven therapists were trained to deliver the treatment to clients fulfilling a diagnosis of alcohol dependence. Network Support Therapy worked on engaging people's social networks in treatments from the very first therapeutic contact. From the twelve cases that completed a six-session intervention, twenty-two network members were engaged at some point in the treatment process including spouse/partner (n=8); daughters (n=4); sons (n=2); sisters-in-law (n=2); friends (n=2); neighbours (n=2); mother (n=1); niece (n=1) (Ellis 1998; Copello et al. 2002). This early work confirmed that it was feasible to train staff to work with social networks and that the intervention was well received by both the focal clients and network members involved. An important issue to emerge from this work was the need to include coherent strategies to work with those clients who had difficulty engaging a social network and this has been included in SBNT. Within SBNT while retaining the overall philosophy of the treatment approach and the focus on the client's environment, a number of strategies are outlined based on social skills approaches to help those clients experiencing difficulties recruiting network members into treatment in order to develop sources of social support for change within their environment.

In relation to the treatment process, Ellis (1998) reported that:

⊙ Relationships between focal clients and network members and among network members themselves became closer (better communication, more frequent contact, more positive contacts, more agreement about the drinking goal for the client, more understanding about each other's point of view about the drinking and its effects etc.).
⊙ Focal clients and network members felt better understood and more supported.
⊙ Focal clients and network members felt more confident about the drinking and more confident that they could cope in the event of relapse.
⊙ Focal clients and network members remained in closer touch after treatment, providing more positive reinforcement for improvement and faster and more effective action in case of relapse.

Ellis' (1998) work provided a solid platform from which to develop SBNT for implementation in the United Kingdom Alcohol Treatment Trial.

EVALUATION OF SBNT

SBNT has been studied as part of a randomised trial for alcohol problems, the UKATT. UKATT constituted the largest trial of psychosocial treatments for alcohol problems conducted in the UK and involved a comparison between SBNT and Motivational Enhancement Therapy (MET). The trial was pragmatic and conducted in a range of alcohol treatment services across the UK. Therapists were selected from the services and trained and supervised in order to deliver the two trial treatments, in which 742 clients were randomly assigned to receive either intervention and were then followed up at the end of treatment (three months) and at twelve months. Results showed that both SBNT and MET led to significant improvements in the main outcomes (number of drinks per drinking day and number of days abstinent from drinking) as well as improved mental health related quality of life and that there were no significant differences in outcomes between the two treatments (UKATT Research Team 2005a). In addition, economic analysis revealed that both treatments were associated with significant cost savings related to health care and criminal justice and there were no differences in cost-effectiveness between the two treatments (UKATT Research Team 2005b).

A further study (Copello et al. 2006b) was conducted with drug users in routine UK services. SBNT was adapted to work with drug users and clients who received SBNT were followed up at the end of treatment. In total, twenty therapists were trained and managed to deliver SBNT to twenty-four drug-using clients as part of the study. Results showed significant before to after improvements in outcome variables including levels of drug use and family related variables such as improved family cohesion, reduced open conflict and increase in overall family satisfaction

SUMMARY SO FAR

The available research evidence and early feasibility work informed the development of SBNT. SBNT brings together elements of network therapy (Galanter 1993a), unilateral family therapy (Thomas and Ager 1993), behavioural couples therapy (O'Farrell and Fals-Stewart 2006), social aspects of the community reinforcement approach (e.g. Sisson and Azrin 1989; Meyers et al. 1996); relapse prevention (e.g. Chaney et al. 1978), coping skills training (Monti et al. 2002), approaches with family and concerned others (Yates 1988; Copello et al. 2000a, 2000b; Howells and Orford 2006) and integrates aspects of these approaches within a unified social treatment approach which has theoretical coherence. The therapist uses a combination of network management skills, education about alcohol and its effects, material on coping, communication and increasing social support and allocates time to plan for the future including dealing with possible lapse or relapse. Information is provided for each topic that is used as part of SBNT to guide the therapist's decision making and to ensure that the network addresses areas of life that are frequently problematic to those drinking excessively. All the objectives that are set should support the overall goal of the client's decreased drinking or abstinence or should work to provide help and support to other network members who should thereby be better able to positively help the client either in the present or in the future. This support can be available for clients attempting to maintain a change in their drinking behaviour or if not successful initially at any time when the client is ready to change.

PHILOSOPHY OF SBNT

Social Behaviour and Network Therapy is a systematic approach based on an understanding of addiction problems which stresses the role of the problem drinker's social environment in supporting attempts to change drinking behaviour and to maintain that change over time. SBNT is not a narrowly prescribed set of techniques that can be mechanically used with all problem drinkers. The approach is based on the notion that a 'social network that supports change' is an essential ingredient and therefore a critical condition necessary for the resolution of addictive behaviour. Implicit within this idea is the notion that the social context within which the problem drinker lives can play a crucial role in determining present and future drinking behaviour. This treatment, therefore, considers the reciprocal relationship between the identified drinker and his or her family, work colleagues and friends and the way in which drinking is both affected by and affects both the problem drinker and the network.

SBNT, as a treatment approach, is therefore concerned with the development and consolidation of this 'social network for change' using as a baseline the social network as it exists for each individual problem drinker at the time of presentation for treatment. For some problem drinkers, with a group of very supportive close family members and friends, the work may involve inviting these people to the treatment sessions and developing plans for action. For other problem drinkers the work may involve creating the conditions for the network to function in a supportive way, where the effects of drinking over time may have strained relationships. Some problem drinkers will have no network. For them, the work may involve creating a network in such a way that what might be achieved by the end of the treatment is the introduction of *one* supportive person for those individuals who were previously totally isolated. We believe that the change inherent in increasing the positive social network of an isolated individual by one person may be extremely significant even if it appears a small step compared with those cases where larger numbers of close relatives and friends are involved during the treatment. An important issue to remember when conducting work based on developing social support is that the quality of the support is the most important factor so that one very supportive person that is reliable and keen to be engaged in supporting the focal client may be better than a larger number of potential network members that are not fully engaged in the process.

Overall, the common aim and your key tasks as a therapist involve creating the necessary conditions in the problem drinker's social network that will facilitate change while at the same time, exploring how to minimise or eliminate those parts of the network that support the continued problematic use of alcohol. The treatment name combines the two central aspects of the work involved: the problem drinker's social behaviour may need to be shaped or modified in order to achieve the above aims, and in the cases where a network is available, work needs to be conducted with the network in a therapeutic way to maximise support for positive change.

Further details as to how specifically this work can be carried out are discussed later within the manual. Prior to that, contrasts between SBNT and other approaches are considered as well as the therapist skills necessary for conducting this treatment.

In conducting this work, we have come across a number of therapists who have raised the question as to who the client is. For those therapists used to working mainly with the individual problem drinker, it is sometimes difficult to see other network members as also clients in their own right, yet this is central to this treatment approach. *Part of the philosophy of the treatment is that every person in the room is receiving a service.* Once the treatment starts, therefore, any person presenting for a meeting and agreeing to be part of the network, becomes a client in their own right and can have access to your service within the structure of the intervention. This can take place whether the person with a drinking problem is present or not. This issue will be discussed further both within the therapist tasks and within the first meeting. Given that both problem drinker and network members are clients, for the remainder of the manual the term *focal person* or *focal client* will be used to denote the person with the drink problem and *network member* to denote those involved in treatment other than the person with the drink problem.

CONTRASTS BETWEEN SBNT AND OTHER TREATMENT APPROACHES

A useful way to clarify some of the key elements of an intervention is by contrasting the intervention to other approaches also used to help people with alcohol problems. In Tables 1, 2 and 3 SBNT is contrasted with three

Table 1 Contrasts between non-directive counselling and Social Behaviour and Network Therapy

Non-directive counselling	SBNT
Individual sessions are held with the client	Sessions if possible involve the focal client and network members
Agenda is set by the client	Therapist sets the agenda for each meeting
Confidentiality: information is not shared outside of the client–therapist contact	Consent is obtained for information to be shared with other network members
Avoids prescription of behaviour	The problem drinker's and network member's behaviour can be explored and changes suggested
Therapist avoids active engagement outside of the individual session	Therapist is active in collaborative attempts to engage network support both within and outside treatment sessions
Individual feelings are explored in depth	Feelings are explored mainly in relation to the present problem and network support
Changes arise from within an individual	Outside influence is central to generate support and sustain change
Avoids giving advice	Advice and feedback offered when appropriate

Table 2 Contrasts between Motivational Enhancement Therapy and Social Behaviour and Network Therapy

Motivational Enhancement	SBNT
The individual's motivation is central to addiction processes. An increase in the individual's motivation to change will increase the likelihood of success	Positive social support for change is central to the addictive processes
Aims to alter the individual's decisional balance and to amplify discrepancy between current use of alcohol and future goals	Aims to maximise outside positive support for change
The therapist discusses motivation as seen by the client	The therapist is an active agent of change within the problem drinker's social environment
Significant others play some role in treatment but are not central	The therapist always attempts to engage significant others that are central to the treatment process
The therapist elicits information from the problem drinker using a number of techniques	The therapist acts as a team leader, leading the team to the attainment of a specific goal

Table 3 Contrasts between family therapy and Social Behaviour and Network Therapy

Family therapy	SBNT
The therapist focuses on trying to understand patterns of interaction	The therapist focuses on interactions related to drinking and positive support. No attempt to understand interpersonal dynamics
The therapist may interpret the dynamics of the group	No interpretation of behaviour
The therapist focuses on resolving pathology	The therapist focuses on developing positive support for change
Drinking is seen as a symptom of dysfunction	Causes of drinking are multiple. Network members are not seen as causing the drink
Change in drinking emerges from indirect work focused on the dynamics of the system	Changes in drinking are influenced directly by the network members' behaviour and responses to the problem drinker
Network members seen as patients and a contributory factor to the problem	Network members seen as potential sources of support, not as part of the problem
Sessions are held with family members	Sessions can include family members or wider members of the social network, e.g. friends

other approaches. These include non-directive counselling, motivational enhancement therapy, and family therapy interventions.

Tables 1, 2 and 3 illustrate some of the key differences between SBNT and more individually based treatments (non-directive counselling and motivational enhancement treatments) as well as family based treatments (family therapy). Some of the main distinctive factors of SBNT involve the focus on social networks that can be wider than the family as well as the specific emphasis of the treatment on *social network support for change* as opposed to individual factors such as motivation or cognitions. In addition, SBNT concentrates on the present and the future and does not emphasise 'dysfunction' or 'pathology', instead aiming to use the social network as a positive force to support and promote a positive change in behaviour. This way of working also introduces changes in terms of aspects of treatment such as confidentiality, active involvement from the therapist sometimes contacting people outside of the treatment sessions and at other times providing advice and where necessary education.

CHAPTER 2

The therapist

A number of the skills required of the therapist when conducting SBNT are similar to those involved in other forms of alcohol treatment. In this manual, we do not cover in detail some of the more basic counselling skills that are used when working with individuals. These are assumed to be within the repertoire of skills available to alcohol practitioners. There are, in addition, a set of new skills that will be necessary for the successful implementation of SBNT. As a therapist you need to be able to develop these skills which are outlined below.

GENERAL SKILLS FOR THE PRACTICE OF SBNT

Think network

One of the most important abilities is to be able to *think network*. This refers to your ability to think, understand or select any aspect of your intervention in a way that constitutes a step towards an increase of positive network support for the focal person. Whereas 'thinking network' may be easier when there is a network of people in the room, the ability to think in this way becomes particularly important for those problem drinkers who may be isolated. An example to illustrate this point involves social skills training. If this type of work is undertaken within SBNT, the focus needs to be on how the focal person can develop the necessary social skills required to approach people in order to incorporate these people into their social network, as opposed to the more general social skills work that might be part of other treatment approaches. In some cases it is even possible that the same skills are developed and worked on within the meeting but the context within which this is done and the purpose are different, e.g. non-verbal communication including body posture, tone of voice and eye contact are explored and developed within the context of approaching a particular person (either known or a new individual) in order to increase positive support for the focal person rather than as a general approach to training someone in social skills. Another example involves the development of communication skills where the focus may involve setting up skill rehearsal and practice of a telephone call to someone from the network with whom the relationship has been strained or writing a letter to a relative that the focal person has not seen for some time, or to a friend or relative explaining the current problems and asking for support. *The emphasis of this work is therefore not on the development of social competence in general but only social competence in relation to the development of positive social support.*

Focus on positive support

The second ability involves sustaining a focus on *positive support* for the focal person. This involves being able to keep a clear focus on opportunities to develop this form of support and to minimise the opposite, i.e. high conflict and problematic relationships. The importance of positive support cannot be overstated. In contrast to other forms of treatment for alcohol problems where the work is carried out essentially through processes centred on the individual focal person, within SBNT the powerful force of change resides within the quality of positive support and behaviour of those around the focal person. An implication of this is that the important change processes are more likely to occur outside the treatment session and sometimes beyond the period of treatment. This may be so, particularly, if through your intervention a coherent and supportive network is established which can continue to support the focal person in his/her goal over time.

The therapist as an active agent of change

As a therapist you are an *active agent of change* focused on the development of positive support for the focal person. This orientation is in sharp contrast to other approaches (e.g. non-directive counselling) and may involve for example telephoning network members on behalf of the focal person, visiting a network member together with the focal person, or writing to potential network members to invite them to the meetings. One question that you should ask yourself throughout the intervention is:

Have I done everything I can to engage supportive network members in the treatment?

The therapist as a task oriented team leader

In the same way as that postulated by Galanter (1993a) in relation to Social Network Therapy, 'the therapist's relationship to the network is that of a *task oriented team leader*, rather than that of a family therapist oriented towards insight'. There is a clear task for the network to work towards, which involves supporting the focal person to attain the chosen goal (abstinence or moderation). Your role as a therapist is to direct and lead the network towards the achievement of the chosen goal. The broad aims of the intervention include: increasing available positive support; improving communication; increasing the use of both social and other community resources to assist in the achievement of the treatment goal; understanding both alcohol problems and relapse; and developing social activities which are alternative to drinking. Unlike other forms of treatment, the goal is not one of exploration of network members' own problems or past experiences or causes of drinking but one of joint working towards a particular task. *This particular way of working should be clearly communicated at the beginning of the treatment to all those involved.*

Planning your sessions in advance

An important aspect of your work as a therapist involves planning your sessions in advance. While to some extent you will need to address specific problems or situations that have emerged at any point during the intervention, you will need to be familiar with the materials to cover in a particular session and how you plan to structure the time. All the above skills are essential to the delivery of SBNT and summarised in Figure 1 by reference to the acronym PLAN.

SPECIFIC TASKS

As a therapist your role involves a number of specific tasks which are outlined below.

Help the focal person to identify his or her current social network

After a thorough discussion and review of the focal person's social network conducted within the first meeting, you will help both the focal

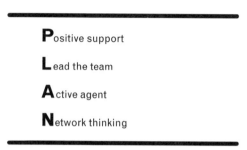

Figure 1 Skills for the delivery of Social Behaviour and Network Therapy

person and those network members present to clarify the current situation and to identify positive people who can be invited to subsequent meetings. The process involved in this task is discussed more fully later in the manual as part of the first session.

Communicating the importance of building network support

It is important to acknowledge that problem drinkers, when they seek help, do not always have a social network that is functioning effectively. In fact when problem drinkers present for treatment the social context within which they exist may range from the person being totally isolated to, at the other end, the person having a range of people who are willing to offer positive support. Whatever the specific situation is for each person, you will need to communicate clearly and positively the importance of the work involved in this treatment that aims to build a positive *social support network for change.*

This task may need to be handled skilfully, given that you might be tapping into an area of significant difficulty in particular for the focal person who is isolated. Some resistance to the idea of this type of work could manifest itself in the focal person denying the relevance of this type of work to the drinking problem. You will need to be clear and communicate the centrality of this type of work as discussed at the beginning of this section.

Engaging the network

As a therapist you will need to play an active role in helping the focal person to identify and invite network members to the meetings. How to carry this out will vary from case to case. Sometimes you may need to write to potential network members, on other occasions you may need to contact them directly by telephone.

Our experience suggests that engaging the network is an ongoing process that is rarely complete after the first session. In some cases, this process forms a significant part of the treatment intervention. The case example below illustrates clearly how work related to engaging the network members does not end early on in treatment but is an ongoing task.

Case example: Richard, Laura and Ikbal

Richard had attended the first meeting on his own and the next two meetings with his girlfriend Laura. During the second meeting Ikbal, a common friend of both Richard and Laura, was identified as a potential network member who could attend some of the sessions. It was agreed that Laura would approach Ikbal and invite her to the meetings. At the following meeting, Richard and Laura came but there was no sign of Ikbal. This issue was discussed and Laura reported that she had not had a chance to talk to Ikbal. It was agreed that this remained an important goal and that Laura should attempt again in the following week. Ikbal worked full time so a late meeting was agreed. The remainder of the meeting was used to discuss coping.

The following meeting Richard arrived on his own but said that Laura and Ikbal were on their way. Minutes later they both arrived. Ikbal described how pleased she was that Richard was trying to tackle his drinking and described her perception of the situation. Ikbal said how she saw herself as an important source of support for Laura and that she had noticed in the past that Richard drinks 'excessively' but was unsure as to how to respond. She was keen to help and be involved. A number of tasks were agreed during that meeting:

- Richard, Laura and Ikbal would go out once during the following week to do something that was not alcohol focused e.g. go bowling or go to the cinema.
- Ikbal's support for Laura was acknowledged and identified as important.
- Richard asked Ikbal to respond to his excessive drinking in any future situation by stating how she felt about his drinking and leaving the situation (i.e. if Richard drunk too much).

Help the whole network identify a common agreed goal for treatment of the alcohol problem

During the early part of treatment it is important that some discussion takes place as a result of which a common goal of treatment is agreed. You may find that different people have different ideas about this goal and these different views will need to be addressed.

In our work so far, we have found that the network members can be very resourceful in terms of both generating ideas and also gently challenging the focal person. Examples of this include relating past experiences when the focal person tried in the past to achieve a particular drinking goal and using these experiences to discuss how difficult it may be to succeed this time. If these interactions are handled well, they can be very useful for the identification and establishment of a realistic goal for treatment.

Set the agenda and follow the structure for each meeting

You will need to be clear about the agenda for each meeting. Each meeting will have an area or topic to cover (e.g. social support, coping, communication), but there will be some variation in relation to the focus of the work. It is not unusual for both the focal person and the network members to wish to discuss a number of issues which are of concern to them. You will need, however, to keep the focus on the task at hand and to clearly explain at the beginning of each meeting what will be covered. This will also involve deciding on the precise content of each meeting.

Empowering the network, promoting cohesion and managing conflict

Those concerned and affected by the problem drinking including family and friends will often be keen to help and may already be trying out strategies of their own. Your task as a therapist is to utilise the network's willingness and preparedness to help and to ensure that the strategies that they use are helpful in supporting and helping the focal person to attain the drinking goal that he/she has chosen. The responsibility for change remains with the focal person and each network member is only responsible for his/her role in helping the person attain and maintain the goal.

Any efforts to change behaviour and maintain this change over time are more likely to succeed when there is network cohesion. Cohesion is increased by promoting a sense of belonging to the network and each member feeling that he/she is able to make a positive contribution to the group's task (ultimately the achievement of the focal person's drinking goal). It is also important to minimise conflict. Throughout the intervention, the focal person is an integral part of the network and should be seen as part of the team. Part of the approach needs to promote the idea that neither the focal person nor other network members are cast in the roles of either being a *victim* or being to *blame* for the problems. The emphasis is on the fact that everyone involved has responsibility for their own behaviour and that the social network is responsible for working together to support both the focal person and each other.

A likely source of difficulty during the meetings involves arguments between network members other than the focal person or network members and the focal person. The arguments may revolve around events that have happened in the past or events that have happened recently. You should remember that this treatment does not involve trying to resolve conflicts of network members other than those directly related to responding to the person's drinking. Nor does it attempt to address or explore any of the problems of individual network members other than those directly related to responding to the person's drinking. If conflicts or other problems arise, you should acknowledge network members' feelings but go on to explain that individual problems cannot be addressed in this setting. *You should re-state that the primary purpose of the meeting is to help and support the focal person in achieving and maintaining the drinking goal.* If the conflict continues you can reflect this back and also explore what effect arguments have on the overall goal and whether or not these arguments help the network to attain their goal. The way that you manage conflict needs to be directive but not confrontational.

Within SBNT we attempted to resolve conflicts by focusing upon two principles. First, we made sure that all points of view were clearly understood by the therapist and that network members were convinced that they had been understood. Second, the therapist was always on the lookout for win-win solutions. Here is an example:

Two network members Phil and Doreen used to drink with the focal person Julian every Thursday night. When Julian's drinking became excessive, they refused to socialise with him and this resulted in a rift. This conflict was resolved by reinstating the habit of going out together every Thursday but to situations such as the cinema or a restaurant where the temptation to drink would be less.

Creating a win-win situation requires that the needs of all parties are clearly understood.

Elizabeth had reached breaking point as her husband's drinking became more and more excessive. Arthur was convinced that he could have two lagers with her on a Saturday night as they used to do last year. She refused. She could not stand his violent argumentative attitude that she associated with alcohol. He wanted a pleasant social evening with a small amount of alcohol. Elizabeth agreed to a six-week experiment. This turned out to be a great success. They both enjoyed the evening out and there was no evidence of violence.

It is important that you reinforce everyone for working as a team together, completing tasks between sessions or in any situation where positive feedback will strengthen the relationship with each other. You should aim to leave members feeling empowered and should act to increase feelings of responsibility and self-esteem.

You should work with a focal person and network as you would work with a team of people who are equal to you. Although you will manage the presentation of information in the sessions the focal person and network are responsible for how they use the information. You should not make decisions for anyone but should act as a consultant and be prepared to challenge any decisions made if necessary. You should communicate the feeling that you are supportive of both the focal person and network and that you understand their situation. The specific tasks that you need to focus on are summarised in Table 4.

Table 4 Therapist tasks when conducting Social Behaviour and Network Therapy

Key tasks
Help the focal client to identify the social network
Communicate the importance of building or developing network support
Promote active engagement of the network
Work towards a common agreed realistic drinking goal
Set agenda and maintain structure
Empower, promote cohesion and manage conflict
Promote realistic hope and optimism

DEALING WITH SETBACKS

Sometimes during the intervention you may find that there are setbacks in terms of the drinking goal or difficulties involving the focal person and other network members. Setbacks should be seen as part of the process towards the resolution of the problem and therefore used as further information and feedback in relation to the progress of the treatment.

A particular type of setback involves the non-attendance of network members following their engagement at previous meetings and agreement that they would continue to attend. When this occurs, you need to explore the reasons behind the non-attendance in depth and if necessary actively attempt to re-engage the absent network members in the treatment. You could contact the network members who did not attend and discuss with them the reasons for this. It is important, however, that this is discussed rather than continuing with the work as if nothing had happened.

A further possible setback involves the non-attendance of the focal person. In cases where a network is involved, the work should focus on re-engaging the focal person in treatment through working with the network members present. This is discussed further within the manual.

CONTACT FROM NETWORK MEMBERS OUTSIDE OF THE MEETINGS

In contrast to other more individual based treatments, in SBNT contact can take place between network members and the therapist between meetings. While you may want to encourage the network member to discuss the concerns or issues at the next meeting of the network, you may find situations where you need to spend some time between meetings exploring concerns and discussing possible strategies. In our experience, although on occasions this need arises, it can be dealt with effectively without taking up too much of the therapist's time.

Case example: Stephen and Linda

During the week, two days prior to the next scheduled meeting, Stephen's (focal person) sister-in-law Linda (a network member who was involved in the treatment) contacted the therapist by telephone. Linda was concerned because she had found out that Stephen had started drinking again and was unsure as to how to respond to the situation. She could not decide whether to confront Stephen about his drinking or to pretend that she knew nothing about it. Through a discussion with the therapist, during which she reviewed different options, Linda decided that she would tell Stephen that she knew that he had been drinking, that she felt frustrated about the fact that he did not approach her prior to resuming drinking and that she wanted to discuss this further at the next meeting in two days' time. She also stated that she was willing to continue to support Stephen's efforts to change.

UNILATERAL WORK WITH NETWORK MEMBERS IN THE ABSENCE OF THE FOCAL PERSON

As previously discussed, in cases where the focal person stops attending, the work can continue with those network members who are willing to continue to meet for the remainder of the treatment contract. In the first instance, work should clearly focus on how the network can continue to support the focal person, including the possibility of re-engaging the focal person in the sessions. Strategies could be discussed and tasks allocated to different members of the group.

Case example: Martin, Ray and Brenda

Martin had attended three SBNT meetings and had engaged his brother Ray and his sister Brenda as network members. On the day of the fourth meeting, Brenda rang the therapist to say that Martin would not be attending and that she felt that there was not much point in Ray and herself attending the meeting without Martin. She clearly sounded upset. In response to the therapist's advice, both Ray and Brenda came to the meeting and discussed the progress achieved to date and their perceptions of why Martin had decided to stop attending. They formulated a plan in order to approach Martin and to ask him to rejoin the meetings. They agreed that Brenda would talk to Martin. Brenda would express her feelings of concern and state how much she would like Martin to think carefully about continuing with the treatment. Later on the same day, Ray would make telephone contact with Martin and communicate a similar message. Martin, Brenda and Ray all turned up for the fifth appointment where time was spent exploring what had happened in the previous week.

This is a particularly powerful way of working that not only aims to re-engage the focal person in a way that would not be possible within an individual focused treatment, but also continues to address the needs of those network members present. This issue is discussed later as part of the first session of treatment.

ADDITIONAL THERAPIST SKILLS

In her evaluation of Network Support Therapy mentioned earlier in this manual, Ellis (1998) interviewed the therapists delivering the intervention and identified a number of skills which were required in addition to a good knowledge of alcohol problems and relapse issues, and counselling and communication skills. The additional skills included the ability to retain neutrality, to create a safe situation for clients and network members, to be a 'referee' who is tactful, non-judgemental and can combine directive and supportive strategies as the situation requires. In addition, therapists noted that the management of a group with a 'shared past' raised different issues to those encountered in other forms of group work where people come together with a particular work agenda but no common shared history.

UNDERSTANDING THE CONTENT OF THE SESSIONS

You should be familiar with and understand the material content of each session. Since many of the sessions may require the use of skill rehearsal or setting up homework tasks, some attention is given below to these two tasks.

Skill rehearsal

Skill rehearsal or role play involves practising situations that involve the use of skills in the context of the session before moving on to use the skills in the real world. Skill rehearsal may be a component of some of the sessions and it is a useful way for both the focal person and other network members to practise and learn new skills. When people first use skill rehearsal they often feel embarrassed or uncomfortable. This should be acknowledged as a normal reaction and you should emphasise that skill rehearsal will get easier with practice. If necessary, you should demonstrate the first exercise. In practice we have found it much easier to avoid the use of words such as 'skill rehearsal' or 'role play' and instead talk about 'having a go at practising a situation'. People tend to find this description less threatening.

Before setting up a skill rehearsal exercise the focal person and network members will be required to think of their own situations and should be able to give descriptions of the scene including where the event takes place, who is there and what is said. There are a number of ways that the focal person and network members can be helped to think of different scenarios.

- First, network members might be asked to recall situations in the past where using the new skill would have been useful, e.g. Friday evening, Martha was at home and felt like a drink but could not bring herself to go to see her neighbour Philip and ask for some support as Martha did not know how to approach the subject.
- Second, the focal person and network can be asked to think of situations that may occur in the near future when using the new skill might be helpful, e.g. Peter meets Simon and realises that he has been drinking but is not sure how to respond to the situation.
- Third, you could suggest situations based on your knowledge of the focal person and network, e.g. Linda wants to approach Jim and ask him to join the network but is not sure how to raise the subject.

A further strategy that may be used is *role reversal*. This might involve:

- modelling a new skill with the focal person, or
- a network member playing the focal person, or
- the focal person and one other network member swapping roles.

Role reversal is useful at times when the focal person or network member is having difficulty using a skill or is pessimistic about a particular approach. When the focal person or network member plays the 'other', they have a chance to observe and experience the effect of the new skill. This can be a powerful way to understand some of the processes involved in interactions between network members and the focal person or among network members themselves. An example of this technique can be seen when a particular person needs to be approached to join the network such as the case of Linda described earlier. Linda can take the place of Jim and experience what it might be like to be asked for help in a clear and assertive manner. Her anticipated fear of how Jim may react can then be discussed.

Homework tasks

Setting homework tasks and reviewing them in the session can be a powerful tool in treatment. To some extent, the type of homework tasks given within SBNT differs from other forms of treatment. Examples of homework tasks include: asking the focal person and network members to discuss and agree the drinking goal between meetings, for the focal person to go out during the week and engage with network members in an activity which is not drink related, for a member of the group to approach and identify a potential network member and talk to him/her about coming to the next meeting.

Compliance with homework tasks can be a problem and there are several steps that you can take to encourage compliance:

1 When an assignment is given out, you should provide a careful rationale and description of the assignment.
2 Ask the focal person and the network whether they can see any problem in completing the assignment and talk about ways that any problems could be overcome.
3 The focal person and the network should be asked to identify a specific time which they could set aside to work on their assignment.
4 You should review assignments at the beginning of the following session.
5 You should acknowledge and discuss any problems that the focal person or the network have with completing assignment tasks.

The main emphasis, however, should be placed on reinforcing the positive aspects of that person's performance. If there are people who did not manage to carry out the tasks assigned, you should discuss with them what could be done to avoid this in the future.

The treatment

GENERAL OUTLINE OF THE CONTENTS OF SBNT

Below is a general outline of the work that is involved in SBNT. This treatment has been developed to take into account the variation between problem drinkers and hence focuses on diverse areas based on a number of identified needs (Copello et al. 2002):

1 The drinking problem may have alienated some or all of the potential network members. A first step in SBNT is to identify who these individuals are and provided the focal person thinks that they will be supportive make contact with them, and invite them to take part in supporting the focal person in his or her efforts to change. How to achieve this is discussed later in the manual.
2 Members of the network may not agree with the focal person or among themselves, about the appropriate drinking goal. An agreed goal should be discussed and negotiated.
3 Network members may have different views about how to support the focal person and how to respond in the event of relapse. An agreed strategy should be negotiated with network members and with the focal person.
4 Network members may have been coping with the drinking problems in ways that they recognise, on reflection, to be counterproductive. They will need discussion and practice about ways of coping, including skill rehearsal and homework.
5 The focal person may not be using network members in a way that is supportive. He or she should be helped to develop ways of using positive network members more effectively (e.g. by contacting network members at times of risk).
6 The focal person and members of his/her social network may have been communicating ineffectively. Together they may plan and practise improved ways of communicating.
7 The focal person and members of his/her network may have been undertaking few joint activities which have been pleasant, and hence the focal person may have little access to activities that are alternatives to drinking. Together they may be helped to plan such activities and to increase their frequency.
8 The focal person may find it difficult to enlist support from network members when relapse occurs. There is a need to develop a shared understanding of the relapse process and to discuss joint strategies for dealing with lapses. This may include the identification of early signs of impending risk for lapse and possible responses to these.
9 In some cases, it may be difficult for problem drinkers to identify anyone who might join a positive network for change and it may be necessary to recruit a 'buddy' (e.g. a former problem drinker or a volunteer worker) who will, for a period of time, perform the functions otherwise served by a natural support network.

10 Problem drinkers, at the time of seeking help, often show a lack of skill in social behaviours necessary to make contact with potential network members and use them effectively. Skills training will then be used: communication skills such as starting conversations, re-establishing contact by telephone with a potential network member, composing a letter to a potential network member, dealing with criticism from a potential network member. As stated previously, the focus of this work will be on engaging potential network members as opposed to general social competence.

A number of tasks become evident from our discussions so far and are included within this treatment. They include:

⊙ identifying and contacting network members
⊙ identifying skills deficits which may be responsible for the failure to mobilise a network and providing appropriate social skills training specifically focused on contacting significant others
⊙ introducing a 'buddy' or an Alcoholics Anonymous sponsor if necessary
⊙ working with a network in order to reach and maintain agreement about the drinking goal and coping strategies or with the aim of improving communication and frequency of pleasant activities
⊙ maintaining the cohesion of the network
⊙ providing a consistent and helpful network response in the event of relapse or the failure of the person with a drinking problem to attend
⊙ identifying further sources of social support for the person with a drinking problem
⊙ planning for the future including how to deal with and respond to the possibility of relapse.

In cases where no network is present, the work should aim to begin to develop this network by identifying and contacting people as illustrated in the following case example.

Case example: Pat

Pat came to the first meeting and following the assessment of his social network, it became clear that he had no friends or relatives. Both his parents were dead, he had no friends and his marriage had ended twelve years ago. The next meeting was spent introducing the concept of meeting new people and identifying places where new people could be met. Pat had been a keen rambler prior to the development of his drink problem and joining a rambler's club was an option. A local club was identified and details were obtained. Communication skills were practised including starting conversations and talking about feelings and listening skills. Once these skills were developed, Pat's homework task involved contacting the club and attending a meeting.

In the case where the network is present but has been significantly strained, the work may need to focus on generating some change if possible or look for alternative supports if the former cannot be achieved.

In cases where there are already a number of network members who are willing to be involved in helping and supporting the focal person, the work should aim to facilitate and develop this process further.

ORGANISATION AND STRUCTURE OF THE TREATMENT

In order to cater for the differences in the problem drinkers presenting for treatment, SBNT has been designed so that the philosophy of the treatment, as described at the beginning of the manual, is stressed as the coherent core central element that unifies all aspects of the intervention.

Figure 2 illustrates the overall structure and potential processes involved in the intervention.

The first and last meetings are common to all cases, the only difference being whether network members (NMs) are present or not at the meetings. The first meeting involves reviewing the social network of the focal person (FP) and the final meeting focuses on preparation for the future.

Three main strands of work emerge from the second meeting onwards. In *cases where network members are present during the second meeting*, the work continues to focus on the network as a whole, e.g. communication, coping, enhancing support and managing relapse focus on everyone present in the room.

In *cases where no network members are present but potential network members (PNMs) are identified*, the work focuses on engaging the PNMs in the meetings, e.g. communication skills are developed to approach and invite PNMs and if necessary to deal with conflict, attempts are made to understand how to reduce coping responses by PNMs that may be preventing them from joining the meetings, support is explored in relation to PNMs and the relapse management plan focuses on seeking support to avoid lapse or relapse.

In *cases where the focal person is totally isolated* and no potential network members are identified, the work focuses on building a social network from scratch, e.g. how to start a conversation with a stranger, how people's coping can interfere with building new relationships, how to build social support and how to use community resources to aid relapse prevention and management.

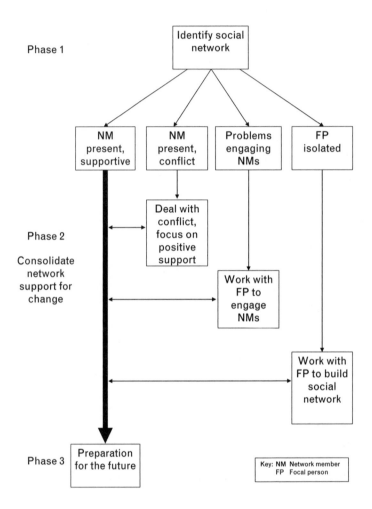

Figure 2 Possible strands of work

The decisional flow chart in Figure 3 has been designed to help you decide which strand to work on. In some cases there will be movement between the different paths and the diagram illustrates some of the decisions that as a therapist you will need to make to refocus the work depending on the needs of each particular client at each point in time during treatment. This allows you as a therapist to develop an individualised treatment plan, yet remain grounded on the philosophy of the treatment approach.

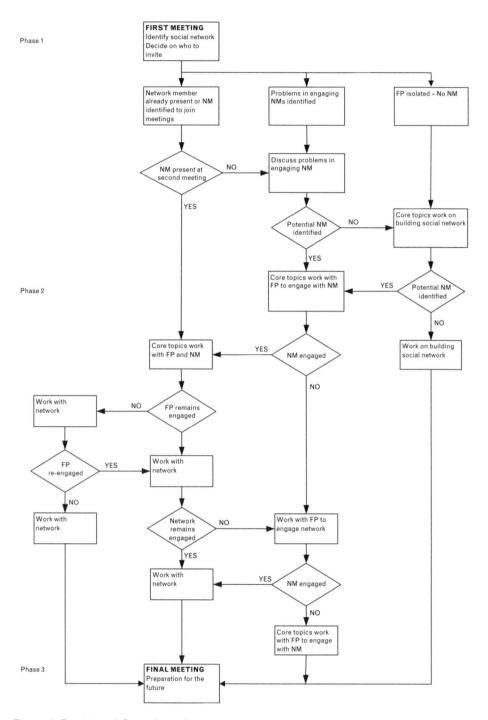

Figure 3 Decisional flow chart: how to make decisions about the focus of treatment

CORE AND ELECTIVE COMPONENTS

The programme is organised as follows: there are three phases in the treatment including:

- ⊙ Phase 1: Introductory session
  Establishing the focal person's social network
- ⊙ Phase 2: Combination of core topics and elective topics
  Building positive support for change
- ⊙ Phase 3: Final session
  Termination and planning for the future

Phase 1 and Phase 3 can both be completed within one session, i.e. the initial and final sessions respectively. Phase 2 as used in our previous research consists of six sessions. All three phases are equally important.

The introductory session, the four core topics and the termination session are provided to all clients. You should spend at least one session on each core topic. Any core topic can be repeated if necessary to complete the schedule. The core and elective topics are summarised in Table 5. The precise content of the sessions will vary according to whether the focal person is on his/her own or with a member of the social network, i.e. as already discussed the sessions are tailored to meet the clients' needs. This combination of core and elective topics has been used in previous studies (e.g. Project MATCH *Twelve Step Facilitation Therapy Manual*: Nowinski et al. 1995) and allows the development of 'individualised treatment plans within broad parameters' (Nowinski et al. 1995: 5). In the case of SBNT, this flexibility needs to accommodate those clients with whom a social network has been engaged in treatment as well as those with whom this is an ongoing focus of the treatment work.

Table 5 Core and elective topics

Core
Communication
Coping
Enhancing social support
Network based relapse management

Elective
Basic information about alcohol
Increasing pleasant and joint activities
Employment
Active development of positive supports
Minimising support for problem drinking

Within each meeting there is also an opportunity to review what has happened in the previous week, what the plans are for the next week, and what actions can those present undertake to support the aim of treatment. The format of the meetings will now be described.

FORMAT OF THE MEETINGS

First meeting

In the first meeting you need to set the scene for the rest of the intervention. Explain the rationale for the treatment approach and undertake a review of the focal person's social network as discussed in detail later in the manual.

Meetings 2 to 7

The remaining meetings are divided into three parts described below.

Part 1: review of progress

(Approximate duration: 10–15 minutes)
The therapist starts the meeting by reviewing the progress over the previous week with particular emphasis on drinking and network support. In cases where a drinking diary has been introduced, it should be reviewed. If no drinking above the agreed goal has occurred, everyone is offered positive feedback. In cases where the focal client is pursuing abstinence, progress in relation to this goal should be reviewed and equally, positive feedback should be given if the goal has been attained. If problematic drinking has occurred, reasons are explored; the goal of treatment is restated and agreed for the next week. This information is taken into account during the next two parts of the meeting.

Homework tasks are reviewed. If the task has been attempted, offer positive feedback irrespective of the result. Explore implications of the results of the homework tasks for the remainder of treatment. Do not set homework tasks until Part 3 later in the session.

Part 2: new material

(Approximate duration: 30 minutes)
In Part 2 you need to move on to cover a specific topic, either core or elective. The topics are described in detail within the manual. Within a topic the material can be adjusted to the particular focal person's situation as long as the presentation remains consistent with the SBNT philosophy. You may combine a core and an elective topic, e.g. information about alcohol (elective) and communication (core).

Part 3: tasks for the next week

(Approximate duration: 10 minutes)
You need to start summarising what has been covered. Look at the week ahead and discuss any homework that may have emerged from the work conducted during Part 2. Discuss any additional strategies or tasks to be undertaken during the week to follow. Agree the appointment for the next meeting. Finish the meeting on a positive note.

Final meeting

The final meeting focuses on preparing for the future and the maintenance of a positive support network in the long term. The detailed content for this meeting is outlined under 'Planning for the future and termination'.

Certain tasks need to be attended to throughout the treatment intervention. Some of these involve the discussion of any contact between therapists and network members that may have occurred outside the meetings, the review of homework tasks, and any further work attempting to increase support for the focal person, including inviting other network members who have not attended sessions previously.

ASSESSMENT

There are a couple of ways to address and incorporate the material needed for SBNT in routine assessment procedures. Services usually have defined routine assessments whose conduct follows a protocol or an agreed procedure. These assessments focus on a range of individual factors, e.g. physical signs of dependence, motivation to change, previous relapse experiences, expectancies about alcohol and its effects. This to some extent reflects the individual focus of service providers. Some teams have incorporated a family focus in their routine work with all clients and therefore include aspects of the first session of SBNT in their initial assessment. An alternative is to encourage teams to add SBNT components to their routine assessments, by identifying the network during the assessment session.

In the research studies that we conducted (e.g. UKATT), SBNT was preceded by a full research assessment that covered some of the aspects already mentioned.

We have found that adopting a family or social focus from the outset is important in that it communicates positively and from the beginning the nature of the approach, the philosophy of the intervention and the high importance given to family and network members when thinking about alcohol problems.

We advocate incorporating information about supportive family members, friends and concerned others in the initial assessment and exploring their suitability for getting involved at the outset, whatever the first steps of treatment involve. In this way, we can take advantage of the benefits of SBNT by increasing the likelihood of treatment engagement through the participation of significant others. Review of the focal client's social network and the identification of the treatment goal can then be addressed at the outset.

FOR WHOM MIGHT SBNT BE UNSUITABLE?

We developed SBNT as an intervention which is applicable to most people seeking help from alcohol services in the UK. Our experience and evaluation suggest that SBNT can be used with all help seekers, with one exception. That exception is where the client wishes to be helped in a different way, usually using a different approach with a strictly individual focus. It is fairly unusual for a help seeker to resist any sort of involvement of concerned others on any level.

Having said that, SBNT does not always require concerned others to attend treatment sessions, provided they are prepared to offer support. Hence distance, for example, is not an impediment if a network member could be engaged via telephone contact or unilaterally through the focal client between treatment sessions.

Another issue to consider and is discussed in more detail later relates to the risk of domestic violence or abuse.

CONFIDENTIALITY

A number of therapists during training raised concerns about confidentiality, particularly given the wider focus of SBNT that involves more than the focal client during treatment. In practice, we have found that, provided therapists follow good practice in relation to confidentiality, this does not create a problem. The agreement to maintain confidentiality is made by all those attending a session so that no information is discussed outside of the sessions unless all present agree that this may be helpful, e.g. when approaching a potential network member who may be helpful but is not fully aware of the extent of the alcohol problem.

Every time a new person joins the network the therapists reminds all those present of the fact that information shared during the meeting is confidential and should not be divulged outside of the meetings unless agreed by all.

WHERE TREATMENT TAKES PLACE

People embarking upon treatment should where possible be given a choice in relation to where the intervention takes place. Our experience to date suggests that seeing people in their homes and at times that do not interfere with normal working hours is conducive to the engagement of supportive networks. Although SBNT can be delivered at the service base and in many agencies, this will be the routine form of delivery, we suggest that home treatment where possible should be considered as an option and an effort should be made to have at least one meeting in the client's own environment.

DEALING WITH THE RISK OF VIOLENCE

A number of families who experience alcohol and other drug problems are at risk of experiencing violence. This is a more common occurrence in those families seeking treatment for substance misuse problems. You will need to make a careful and thorough assessment of the risks of violence and domestic abuse in each case. In cases where this risk is identified, it is important to deal with any risks before embarking upon the intervention.

If the focal client is a perpetrator of domestic abuse, information can be offered on perpetrator programmes (Galvani 2007). If, on the other hand, the focal client is the victim of abuse, you can offer information on support agencies. A plan to deal with violence should be discussed openly. This plan should be very specific and should include establishing whether there is a potential threat of impending violence, specific help that will be requested from identified members of the social network including other family members, where to go for safety in case of an emergency, and what needs to be done in order to avoid being subjected to physical or sexual violence. Most people experiencing violence need time to think about their options although in certain cases prompt action may be required. If you are working as part of an agency or service, you need to be familiar with the policies in relation to responding to violence.

Pay particular attention to issues of violence and domestic abuse when discussing the social network and potential network members. Do not involve people in the network if there is a suspicion of serious violence or abuse. A fuller discussion of the issue of domestic violence in network therapies is discussed by Galvani (2007).

THE NEXT SECTIONS

The following sections of the manual describe in more detail the contents of the meetings during all three phases of treatment. The contents of phase 1, phase 2 and phase 3 are followed by a description of the elective topics. Each section describes some of the general principles related to each area and suggestions are made as to how the material can be used with the focal person and the network together or with either the focal person or network alone in conducting unilateral work. The treatment structure allows for a certain degree of flexibility in the use of the material and for clinicians to apply their judgement and use their experience. Remember, however, that you need to follow a treatment plan under-pinned by the crucial aim of developing or consolidating *social network support for change.*

PART 2

Core components of SBNT

Phase 1: Identifying the social network

THE FIRST SESSION: SETTING THE SCENE

RATIONALE

Central to the philosophy of Social Behaviour and Network Therapy is the notion that to give the best chance of a good outcome, a person with a serious drinking problem needs to enlist the support of one or more people who will help the person to abstain or significantly reduce drinking and to maintain this new drinking level. This group of significant others can be regarded as a 'social network for change'. *Identifying and enlisting the focal person's social network and setting the scene for the remainder of the intervention is the central focus of the Phase 1 of treatment and the work to be conducted during the first meeting.*

Given that SBNT stresses the importance of the involvement of significant others from the outset, it is important that in most cases where the focal person brings someone with them to this first session, this person can be involved in the treatment straightaway. If this is not the case, work in the first session is conducted with the focal person in order to achieve the following aims.

AIMS OF THE FIRST SESSION

1 To communicate to the focal person (and any network members if present), the philosophy of the treatment and the format of future sessions.
2 To discuss the drinking goal for the intervention with the focal person (and any network members present) and to attempt to reach agreement about the goal with those present.
3 To conduct a thorough review of the focal person's current social network including those who may offer positive support for change and those who may continue encouraging problematic drinking. Decisions need to be made about whom to invite and how to approach them.
4 To communicate clearly the fact that anyone from the network can continue to attend all treatment sessions even if other members of the network decide to drop out. This

includes the scenario when the focal client with the drinking problem decides to stop attending and hence the sessions can, and should if necessary, continue with network members in the absence of the focal client with the drinking problem.

CONTENT

There are three main tasks for you to work on in this first meeting. These are:

1 Explaining the treatment philosophy and the rationale that will guide the intervention
2 Reaffirming the drinking goal and introducing if necessary the drink diary (Appendix 1)
3 Conducting a review of the focal person's social network and developing a clear understanding of the focal person's current situation.

Explaining the treatment philosophy

An example of how to describe the aims and rationale for the treatment is given below:

Therapist: The treatment which we are about to embark upon is a socially based treatment. It is based on the idea that the chances of success will be far greater for someone with a serious drinking problem when he/she can enlist the support of one or more people who will help him/her to abstain or significantly reduce drinking and most importantly, to maintain this new abstinence or drinking level. The treatment will consist of one hour sessions that we will plan out now. Today I would like to talk to you about who you think, in addition to us, may be able to offer help and support. We may wish to invite some people who are not with us today to become network members. One particular advantage of this treatment is that even if the person who is drinking excessively decides to stop attending, other members of the network can still continue to meet together with the therapist for the remainder of treatment in order to continue to provide positive support for change to the person who is attempting to change. We need, however, to agree this way of working in principle and make sure that everyone is happy with this.

Allowing plenty of time for questions and discussion

The issues raised above might generate some discussion, particularly if the focal person feels uneasy about other people meeting to talk about him/her while he/she is not present. Ellis (1998) in her evaluation of Network Support Therapy found that all clients and network members involved in her study approved the idea of unilateral meetings in the absence of the person with the drinking problem if the need arose during treatment. We also found little objection in the United Kingdom Alcohol Treatment Trial where the largest number of SBNT cases has been evaluated. It is very important that the purpose of the unilateral meetings is discussed until everyone is clear about the reason behind the continuation. The most powerful reasons are twofold. First, research evidence shows that unilateral approaches can have beneficial outcomes in relation to the drinking problem. Second, the problem does not go away for those closely involved and hence they need to continue to think about ways of responding and dealing with their own experience of stress. Note that the possibility of unilateral work is perhaps a departure from more traditional practice. Before embarking upon the first session, you will need to be very clear about this way of working to allow you to communicate it in a similarly clear way to the focal person and his/her network.

An alternative scenario may involve problem drinkers who cannot identify anyone to be invited to the sessions. You will need to distinguish whether this arises from difficulties communicating with those close to the focal person or because of social isolation. In both cases it becomes important to stress the aim of SBNT in terms of developing positive support. An illustrative example is described below.

Therapist: It sounds from what you are saying that you cannot think of anyone that you can invite to the meetings. In this case, our work needs to focus on how to build positive support for you either by finding ways of approaching some of the people that you have mentioned and with whom your relationship is difficult at present or thinking of meeting new people.

Reaffirming the drinking goal

At some stage during the first meeting you will need to turn your attention to the drinking goal. If the goal is abstinence, this should be clearly agreed and discussed. If the goal is moderation then an acceptable level of drinking should be decided upon. The goal set should prescribe types of drinks, number of drinks and where the focal person will drink.

If a goal of moderation is chosen, you will also need to introduce the drink diary (see Appendix 1). The diary will be used by the focal person for the remainder of the treatment. The drinking goal should be reviewed at every meeting and progress should be checked by reference to the drink diary.

Identifying who can be included in the social network

In some cases, the drinking problem has alienated some or all of the potential network members. A first step in SBNT is to identify who these individuals are, make contact with them, and invite them to take part in supporting the focal person in his/her efforts to change. Copello et al. (2002) found that people who constitute a positive network for change need to:

⦿ be readily available to the focal person, particularly at times of high risk of relapse
⦿ have a positive relationship with the focal person and be an advocate for him or her
⦿ be in agreement with the focal person about the drinking goal (abstinence or moderation)
⦿ be prepared to be firm but kind with the focal person, encouraging him or her to continue to complete the course of treatment and to continue to work towards the agreed drinking goal
⦿ agree to continue to meet with the therapist and other members of the network in the event of the focal person failing to attend
⦿ work with other members of the network, during treatment and afterwards, in order to develop and maintain a consistent, agreed policy with regard to maintenance of drinking change and relapse prevention.

Network members should be people that the focal person trusts and preferably who have known him/her for some time. The network should *not* include:

⦿ people who have alcohol or drug problems themselves or indeed have shown in the past that they promote and/or support problematic drinking
⦿ people who have a superior or inferior relationship in terms of power to the focal person, e.g. managers at work.

Where people are under the age of 16, the therapist needs to take a view about their maturity, involvement already and the complexity of the relationship. Proceed with caution.

Where possible you should aim to include both men and women and people from different generations. The network can involve any number of people. Three or four is a useful number as it is enough to include people from several areas of the focal person's life without creating a group that is so large that it is likely to become unmanageable. In some of our work, considering cases where networks have been engaged we have found the average of network members involved in treatment to be 1.8, in addition to the focal person, with cases ranging from networks of one to networks of four members present at some point during the intervention.

As already mentioned, network members included partners or spouses, daughters, sons, mothers, nieces, sisters-in-law, friends and neighbours. In practice, networks vary greatly in size and composition. It is not essential that networks are large. Remember that one network member alone may make a very important difference to the focal client.

Network members should have no other 'hidden' agenda of their own aside from supporting the focal person's abstinence or decrease in drinking. The membership of the network is a matter of negotiation between the therapist and the focal person. As a therapist you should be prepared to discuss and explore problems with the focal person if you think that someone is unsuitable or if you think that a person suggested might try to undermine the treatment.

Conducting a review of the focal person's social network

In order to decide whom to invite to the sessions, a review of the focal person's current social network needs to be conducted. Sufficient time should be allocated to this task as the process of discussion and selection of the network members in itself can be very important. (Some examples of social networks are illustrated later within this session outline.) As a therapist, you should encourage the focal client and those present (in cases where there are network members already engaged) to think about all the significant people in the focal person's current social network. A network diagram such as the ones illustrated in the case examples that follow could aid this process and should always be conducted at the first meeting. You can encourage the discussion through the use of specific questions, such as 'When did you last see X?' 'What does she think about your drinking?' 'Does Y drink himself?' If this exercise is carried out well, by the end of it, you should be familiar with the social network surrounding the focal person and feel that you have some knowledge about each one of those recorded in the diagram, their relationships to the focal person, and their views or attitudes towards the problem. When constructing a network diagram at this stage, make sure that every person in the focal client's social network is included, not just those people perceived to be supportive. You need a full picture of the focal client's network in order to proceed. Make sure you have had some practice and experience in developing and drawing a social network diagram before you use this technique with focal clients. We have found that eliciting and drawing a social network diagram in this way can be a very powerful and informative exercise when conducted systematically, sensitively and thoroughly.

One possible way of introducing the idea of social networks and building up a picture relevant to your focal person is illustrated below:

Therapist: A useful way to gain an overall picture that will then help us to decide who will support you is to think about those people with whom you are involved on a day-to-day basis or those people from whom you feel you gain support even if you only see them occasionally. Sometimes, because of your drinking, relationships might have become strained and distant. It is also important to consider those with whom this has happened as this treatment might provide you with an opportunity to contact them and rebuild important relationships, particularly if you feel that they will be helpful in the future. The best way to get an overall view of your social network is by drawing a network diagram.

Understanding the focal person's current situation

Following the introduction, you need to draw a diagram (examples of these diagrams can be seen in the case examples) with the focal person and any other person present in that session. Once important people have been identified, you should encourage those present to think about the suitability of each individual for network involvement and to think carefully about the best way to approach network members, particularly if their relationship has been problematic. As a therapist, you should act as a resource and be actively involved in assisting the focal person and others present in the process of inviting network members. This might involve telephone contact or writing to potential network members inviting them to attend the next session.

A possible option is to write to a potential network member. Below is a sample letter that could be used to invite identified network members.

Dear ....,
I am writing to you on behalf of .... who has approached us in order to receive help to tackle his/her alcohol problem. In order to assist .... we need your help.

The treatment that .... will receive involves not just the person with the drinking problem but those close to them as well. One important reason for this is that when someone develops a drinking problem the chances of abstaining/significantly reducing the drinking are greatly improved by enlisting positive support and help from those close to him/her. We therefore invite *key* people in the person's social network to join the treatment sessions.

.... feels that you are someone whom he/she would very much like to be involved in his/her treatment and hence I am writing to invite you to attend our meeting which will take place on .... the .... of .... at ....

If you feel that you would like any further information please do not hesitate to contact me on .... I would also be grateful if you could confirm whether you are able to attend the meeting.

I look forward to meeting you on ....

A further issue to consider is that this may be the first time that you will become aware of people in the social network who maybe supporting or encouraging problematic drinking. You will need to discuss each one of these cases in detail and establish in what way this support for drinking operates and what is the current relationship between the focal person and those in the social network supportive of drinking. You may need to devote some time to deal with this issue in later sessions. One of the elective topics focuses on this area. In SBNT, this work is attempted once positive support has been built in previous meetings. The reasons for this are twofold:

- The focal person will find it easier to disengage from those supporting problematic drinking if alternative sources of positive support are available.
- Network members can play a powerful role in helping the focal person to disengage from sources of support for problem drinking.

The following statement made by a man with an alcohol problem receiving Social Behaviour and Network Therapy illustrates the point:

We was having problems with people coming round the house: there was one person in particular. We needed to keep them away. If my wife answers the door she can tell him where to get off . . . I hadn't been able to tell him to go away before, but now I can.

Once you have identified who will be invited to attend meetings and drawn the network diagram, you need to indicate in the diagram all those members of the focal person's social network that will be invited to join in the treatment. The diagram needs to be used at each meeting as a reference to check on progress.

CASE EXAMPLES

Four case examples are described below to illustrate the varied types of networks that have emerged as part of our work and some of the issues raised by each particular case.

Case study: Michael's social network

Michael was a 37-year-old man with a twelve-year history of heavy drinking. At the time of the initial assessment Michael was drinking 4 to 5 litres of cider every day. Michael came into contact with alcohol services following a referral from the casualty medical officer. Michael had agreed in principle to invite his girlfriend Maria to the meetings but had not managed to organise this. The therapist asked Michael if he could contact Maria directly. Michael agreed and therefore the therapist contacted Maria by telephone. Maria was expecting the phone call and was keen to attend the next meeting. At the next meeting the principles of the treatment were explained and emphasis was placed on the possibility of continuing to work even if Michael decided not to come to the meetings. The remainder of the first meeting focused on reviewing Michael's social network.

Michael's social network was explored and is illustrated in Figure 4.

- *Mother*: Michael felt that his mother was difficult to talk to and he did not feel that he wanted to talk to her about his current difficulties.
- *Maria*: Michael's girlfriend for the last five years. She has been with Michael and the relationship has continued despite Michael's drinking. She was already present at the initial meeting.
- *Anne*: A friend of Michael's from university. Michael has some contact with her but the contact is very sporadic. He is not keen to involve her as he feels that it may be difficult for Anne and Maria to work together.
- *Gregg*: A friend of Michael who has been unwell himself so Michael is not keen to involve him.
- *Drinking companions*: A range of people whom Michael drinks with in the pubs. Michael felt that they were not real friends and that he needed to distance himself from them.
- *James*: A friend of Maria. He works locally and is aware of the problem. He has helped before. He is caring but firm and both Michael and Maria felt that it would be useful to involve James at some stage in treatment.

The review of the network in this case was carried out with Michael and Maria. Both were involved in the discussion, which was very informative. Both agreed that James would be helpful but felt that he needed to be approached by one of them in the first instance. It was agreed that Michael would do this as a homework task and report back at the next meeting. Michael was successful in engaging James at a later meeting.

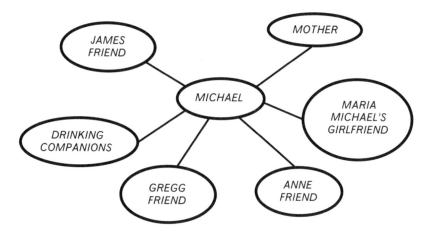

Figure 4 Michael's network diagram

This case illustrates:

⊙ The value of reviewing the network with Michael's girlfriend.
⊙ The flexible approach that may be required when inviting other network members. This can be seen both by reference to the way in which Maria was approached by the therapist and the way in which the approach to James was organised as a homework task.
⊙ The importance of describing the principles of treatment and in particular the fact that meetings can continue with network members in the absence of the person with the drinking problem.

Case study: Margaret's social network

Margaret was a 56-year-old woman referred to the alcohol service because of her excessive consumption of alcohol. During the first meeting her social network was discussed. A number of people emerged as important and are illustrated in Figure 5.

⊙ *Grant*: Margaret's son who is 36 and currently living with his friends. Margaret has a good relationship with Grant.
⊙ *Sophie*: Margaret's sister who knows about the problem and lives locally. Sophie has been very supportive in the past. She has two school-age children and Margaret feels that she may find it difficult to come to meetings.
⊙ *Amy*: Margaret's mother. She knows that Margaret has had an appointment for something related to her health but she is not fully aware of Margaret's problem. Amy is very supportive of Margaret generally and lives locally.

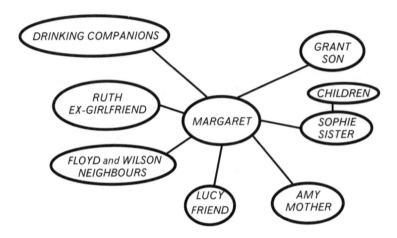

Figure 5 Margaret's network diagram

- ⊙ *Lucy*: A close friend of Margaret and someone who has been very helpful and supportive in the recent past. Lucy is aware of the drinking problem and Margaret would like to invite Lucy to the meetings. Lucy is an accountant and works full time so an evening meeting will need to be arranged.
- ⊙ *Floyd* and *Wilson* are Margaret's next door neighbours. They know about the problem and have been very supportive in the past. An example of their attempts to help is illustrated by the offer to keep Margaret's hamper that she had bought to give to someone as a present so that Margaret is not tempted to drink the alcohol in it. Margaret would like to involve one of them at the meetings.
- ⊙ *Ruth*: Margaret's ex-girlfriend. The relationship is finished and she has not been in touch with her for about two months. Margaret does not want to have any further contact with Ruth at present.
- ⊙ *Drinking companions*: There are a number of people with whom Margaret drinks alcohol but a number of them were friends of Ruth. There was some discussion as to the role of these people in the maintenance of Margaret's alcohol problems.

Margaret was keen to invite both Lucy and Wilson to the next meeting. It was decided to have the next meeting at Margaret's home as it would make it easier both for Lucy and Wilson to attend. Margaret was given a drink diary to complete during the next few days. Both Lucy and Wilson were present at the following meeting.

In the case of Margaret it was evident that she did not wish to involve someone from her family. This was accepted and the possibility of inviting someone to a meeting later if this was seen as helpful was discussed. The choice of network members is negotiated by therapist and focal client but the focal client takes the lead, as the network members need to be perceived as supportive.

Case study: Stephen's social network

Stephen was a 34-year-old man with a fourteen-year history of heavy alcohol consumption. During the past six years, Stephen's drinking had escalated to a point where it caused problems in his marriage, which ended in divorce. Stephen was in danger of losing his job as an advertising manager of a large firm.

Stephen had agreed to invite his brother Jim to the first session. However, due to work commitments, it turned out that his brother could not attend any further sessions but was happy to explore with Stephen the possibility that other members of the family or friends might be invited to attend future sessions.

Stephen's social network was explored and it is illustrated and described in Figure 6.

- *Ken*: Stephen's elder brother. Ken had to some extent distanced himself from Stephen's drinking problems. Stephen did not think Ken would want to get involved and really did not want to invite him.
- *John*: Stephen's younger brother. John had been very supportive at times of difficulty with the drinking problem but was increasingly feeling 'fed up' with him and unlikely to take time off work to attend.
- *Jim*: Stephen's younger brother. Jim had been supportive in the past and would like to attend again but because he travels away from home on business most weeks, this would be difficult.
- *Sarah*: Stephen's ex-wife. Stephen did not feel that he could talk to her about his drinking and did not want to invite her to the sessions.
- *Angela*: John's girlfriend. Angela had been very concerned about Stephen and worried about the increasing distance between the two brothers. Stephen would like to invite Angela to the meetings.
- *Linda*: Jim's wife. She had helped Stephen a great deal when Stephen had become very ill through drinking and Jim thought that Linda would

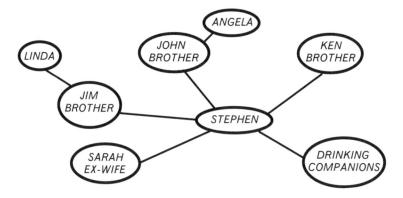

Figure 6 Stephen's network diagram

be keen to help by attending the meetings. Stephen agreed that he would like to invite Linda.

⊙ *Drinking companions*: This group included work colleagues and other people that Stephen had met in the pubs he frequented. This group of people was not seen as particularly supportive in his attempts to stop drinking.

The review of the network was carried out in this case by the focal person and one of his three brothers. Both Stephen and Jim felt that it would be good to ask Angela and Linda if they would like to attend future meetings and they agreed to speak to them individually. Angela and Linda were approached and joined the treatment sessions from then on.

This case illustrates a different network composition including Stephen's sisters-in-law. The case also illustrates the importance of discussing carefully and in detail each network member, their relationship to the focal person and attitudes towards the drinking behaviour.

Case study: Maria's social network

Maria came for treatment of her long-standing alcohol problem. She was 48 years of age and had in the past been married to a man who also consumed alcohol heavily and was physically violent towards her. It became clear early on in the first session that Maria was fairly isolated and had little contact with other people. Maria's social network was explored and is illustrated and described in Figure 7.

⊙ *Rita*: Maria's mother. She is elderly and Maria has not spoken to Rita about her drinking problem. Maria felt that she did not want to approach her mother to discuss her difficulties.

⊙ *Thomas*: Maria's son who is 18 and currently living at home. Maria did not want to involve Thomas in the meetings.

Maria could not identify any other people who she could include in her social network. Maria felt, however, that this was an important factor in her difficulties with her drinking and felt that she wanted to work towards building a network of supportive people.

Figure 7 Maria's network diagram

Maria and the therapist agreed on a number of areas that would be covered during the treatment sessions. These included communication skills, in particular starting conversations and approaching potential network members as well as talking to Thomas about her problems, employment seeking (as Maria wanted to return to some form of employment and this was seen as important in expanding her social network) and learning other ways of developing positive support from the community.

As the meetings progressed it became clear that Maria found it very difficult to talk to Thomas about her alcohol problem because she was worried about his reaction, given that he had suffered significant disruption at home arising from Maria's and her ex-husband's alcohol consumption. Maria felt that she would not be able to handle Thomas' criticisms. Having identified this issue, skills to deal with criticism and to talk about feelings were explored and practised through skill rehearsal. Once Maria felt confident, her homework task involved approaching Thomas and talking about her problems with alcohol and making a specific request for his support.

AFTER THE FIRST SESSION

What you need to do at the end of the first session

At the end of the first meeting you will need to develop a plan for the rest of the intervention. The clearest way to understand the network is as a continuum ranging from:

⊙ one extreme where the person is isolated or the network is experienced as unhelpful, to
⊙ the other extreme where the network is engaged in a very helpful way.

Your aim for the treatment is to work towards the latter extreme of the continuum as this will maximise the chances of success for the focal client in the present and future. For some problem drinkers, for example, the work may initially need to focus on identifying potential network members. Subsequently you may need to work collaboratively with the focal person to attempt to engage a supportive person. Finally, you may create the conditions towards the end of the treatment where discussion of the future with one new network member that you have managed to engage becomes possible at the last session.

Two possible lines of work will emerge from your review of the network. First, for those with no network (or in some cases with no other network than those supportive of drinking) the tasks need to focus on how to develop a positive supportive network by *identifying and approaching potential network members or building a network from scratch*. This constitutes what we call unilateral work with the focal person in order to involve the network. Note that the building of a positive support network takes precedence over any work aimed at reducing the negative impact of those supportive of drinking. The rationale behind this (as already discussed) is that the person with the drinking problem is more likely to be able to resist the pressure from others and also distance him/herself from people who encourage drinking if the person has access to alternative sources of positive support.

Second, for those with a network that can be engaged early in treatment, the work should focus on *developing network support and cohesion* with those present in the meetings.

Later on in treatment a further option may emerge, involving unilateral work with the network members in cases where the focal person stops attending sessions.

The treatment plan is to be agreed with the client and network members present and should roughly specify any important areas to cover in addition to the core topics. The plan should allow some flexibility, given that as indicated in the decisional flow chart (Figure 3) the situation can change during Phase 2. Below is a summary of the tasks relevant to each one of these broad scenarios.

Unilateral work with the problem drinker in order to involve the network

⊙ Identifying possible sources of positive support for the drinking goal.
⊙ Practising communication skills including starting conversations, receiving criticism and approaching people and making requests such as communicating the need for support or more specific ones such as asking the person to join the network.
⊙ Carrying out homework tasks including approaching, telephoning or writing to potential network members.
⊙ Reviewing the impact of drinking upon others, how other people cope and how this may have affected their lack of involvement (e.g. by withdrawing from the person with the drinking problem).
⊙ Enhancing social support networks.

Working with the focal client and the network

⊙ Building cohesion by developing a common understanding of drinking problems and a shared goal for treatment.
⊙ Identifying the tasks that can help the achievement of this goal.
⊙ Developing and practising effective ways of communicating.

⊙ Exploring the different ways in which the network responds or copes with the focal person and development of alternative coping strategies.
⊙ Developing further support for both the focal person and the network members.
⊙ Creating the conditions for the continuation of positive network support in the future.

Unilateral work with the network in the absence of the problem drinker

⊙ Re-engaging the focal person in treatment.
⊙ Coping with the circumstances arising from the focal person dropping out of treatment.
⊙ Supporting the focal person if his/her situation changes in the future and he/she is more able to change.

The following sections cover in more detail the material (core and elective topics) that can be used in individual sessions in order to carry out the above tasks.

Phase 2: Core topics

Phase 2, as already discussed, involves a combination of core and, if necessary, elective topics. The core topics include communication, coping, enhancing social support and network based relapse management. These are described in the following sections.

CORE TOPIC: COMMUNICATION

THE IMPORTANCE OF COMMUNICATION IN SBNT

Communication skills are central to Social Behaviour and Network Therapy. How people communicate influences interactions that can become problematic when a serious alcohol problem develops. The focal person with the drinking problem may be having difficulties communicating with people as a result of the impact of the drinking problem on relationships. Furthermore, when people are together, communication may be poor or indeed increase the amount of conflict. Another challenge involves developing ways to help people communicate the strong feelings that are experienced when a serious alcohol problem affects a social network or when a focal person relapses after a period of good progress. In line with the overall philosophy of SBNT it is important that the orientation of this work is positive and the therapist tries to encourage and promote positive ways of communicating and dealing with problems.

Communication skills are therefore relevant both in cases where a social network is involved and present in the sessions and in those cases where the person is actively being helped to build up a positive support network. The focus of the work will be different in the two types of situation and the possible range of options to be used is included as part of this core topic. A number of options focus on engaging potential network members for cases where you need to spend time on this.

When conducting the communications session you may be faced with *four* possible scenarios:

- a focal client who is isolated
- a focal client who has identified potential network members but does not currently have any engaged in providing positive social support
- a focal client with network members present but there are some current difficulties with communication about the alcohol use
- a focal client with network members present who are communicating positively.

The focus of the work for the communications session will need to be adapted depending on the particular circumstances you encounter.

HELPING A FOCAL PERSON WHO IS ISOLATED

The focal person may be isolated for a variety of reasons, for example a prolonged period of alcohol use may have resulted in a very limited social network developing over time or perhaps the focal person may not have the confidence or social skills needed to build social support. This can be a particularly challenging scenario for a therapist.

The focus of this session is to explore thoroughly potential future network members who may be able to offer positive social support. This may be achieved by reviewing the network diagram with the focal client and being very active in suggesting people who may be able to become engaged in the treatment. It is very important for the therapist to convey optimism to the focal person about the possibilities of developing a positive social network to help increase their confidence and continue engagement with SBNT.

It may be particularly helpful to look at self-help groups such as Alcoholics Anonymous, which can offer high levels of easily accessible support. AA for example offers 24-hour advice and support for abstinence as well as positive role modelling through mentoring. As a therapist, you can offer to contact a group member or potential sponsor and be active in arranging a meeting during the session or alternatively support the focal person in doing so. There are other befriending organisations which may be helpful when beginning to build a social network.

The session could then focus on skills used in starting conversations and examining any concerns the focal person may have. Skill practice can be helpful in these circumstances and lead to increased confidence and self-efficacy. A homework task could be to attend a local AA meeting and feedback the outcome at the next session.

HELPING THE FOCAL PERSON APPROACH POTENTIAL NETWORK MEMBERS

This first section deals with the necessary work to be conducted with the focal person in order to involve the network. The key aspect of this work is to focus on specific tasks that will help to build the network by identifying:

⊙ who might constitute a potential network member
⊙ what are the necessary skills to communicate to this person the need for his/her support and invite him/her to join the meetings.

This emphasis stands in contrast to the general social skills training approach which aims to build up skills to be used in a wider range of situations.

A number of skills are needed when trying to build a positive support network. This is the case both in relation to approaching new people but also communicating feelings or receiving criticism from people with whom the relationship has been strained. The contents of this section describe a number of skills which can help the focal client. You will need to follow three steps.

⊙ Step 1 involves helping the focal client to identify who the potential network member is, e.g. mother, son, friend, befriender.
⊙ Step 2 involves establishing through a discussion with the focal client which strategies will need to be used in order to approach the potential network member.
⊙ Step 3 involves picking up from the following menu the necessary skills to be used with the focal person based on the needs already identified.

You will need to adapt the material depending on need. Some of the skills, for example, could be used to approach someone that the focal person has not spoken to for a long time, and you may want to use this scenario for both skill rehearsal and the homework exercises. The menu includes the following:

⊙ re-establishing contact by telephone
⊙ composing a letter to a network member
⊙ starting conversations
⊙ receiving criticism
⊙ talking about feelings and listening skills.

Each one of these is discussed in more detail below.

RE-ESTABLISHING CONTACT BY TELEPHONE

The telephone can be a useful tool to re-establish contact in particular with those network members who live at a distance from the focal person. As already discussed, as a therapist you need to be actively engaged in the process of developing a positive support network for the focal person. In some cases you may identify a network member with whom communication has recently been poor. A possible way forward is to help the focal person to make contact with this network member by telephone.

Skill guidelines

Identify the person to whom the telephone call will be made. Ask the focal person to describe him/her to you in terms of the relationship, his/her attitude to the focal person's drinking and his/her past response to the drinking problem.

Agree with the focal person the importance of making contact within the context of SBNT. Identify some of the difficulties that might arise when contacting this person, for example he/she may be cold and distant, he/she may not be keen to talk.

Discuss systematically and in detail how the person is to be approached. You can use some of the skill guidelines discussed later in this section under receiving criticism and talking about feelings and listening skills. Develop a plan for the conversation including, for example:

- recognising the lack of contact
- acknowledging past difficulties
- making a specific request
- ending on a positive note.

Practise through skill rehearsal the conversation with the focal person. You can take the role of the network member and in addition use role-reversal to give the focal person an opportunity to think carefully about the best way to approach the subject.

Ask the person to make the telephone call, preferably during the meeting. Offer your help if necessary by dialling and talking to the network member and introducing the discussion.

Alternatively, if it is not possible to make the telephone call during the meeting, set this as a homework task to be reviewed at the next meeting. Once initiated, continue to work on this task, do not abandon it.

COMPOSING A LETTER TO A NETWORK MEMBER

Writing a letter can also be a powerful way of approaching network members. Letter writing offers the chance to think more carefully about what the focal person wants to communicate; it also allows you to guide this communication.

Skill guidelines

Identify the person who needs to be approached. Ask the focal person to tell you about him/her and describe his/her attitude and past response to the drinking problem.

Agree with the focal person on the importance of making contact within the context of SBNT. Spend some time discussing the content of what needs to be communicated. Plan the structure of the letter in terms of:

- ⊙ *Initial paragraph*: acknowledge the lack of contact, anticipate surprise at being written to and if necessary communicate some of the current circumstances leading to the focal person writing the letter.
- ⊙ *Middle paragraph*: the middle paragraph can focus on the important themes to be communicated. Acknowledge the past support provided by the person, communicate how positive this has been and how important it might be to re-establish contact and a supportive relationship, and make a specific request, e.g. to meet sometime in the future, invite the person to join a future meeting.
- ⊙ *Final paragraph*: restate the importance of re-establishing contact and end on a positive note.

If possible compose the letter and write it during the meeting and ensure that the focal person posts the letter straightaway. If this is not feasible or practical, you could set the writing of the letter as a homework task. Offer as much support as you can in order to help the focal person achieve the aim of sending the letter to the network member.

Other forms of communication can also be used, e.g. email contact or talking through Skype. As further and more sophisticated forms of communication are developed, you may be able to encourage focal clients to use these to contact potential network members, even when they live far away. Whether via email or ordinary mail, the same principles discussed apply when attempting to approach someone. It is the content of the approach that is the key and will determine whether the approach is successful.

STARTING CONVERSATIONS

Isolation, for some focal clients, may result from avoidance of socialising or meeting people underlined by a difficulty in making conversations. This avoidance is likely to prevent people from developing a positive social support network and lead to loneliness and isolation that may place the focal person at risk for continued problem drinking.

Often people who drink heavily find themselves mixing with others who also drink heavily. When people reduce their drinking or stop, they may feel lonely at first and miss friends. This may also have resulted from your work in helping the focal client identify and avoid those supporting problematic drinking. Focal clients may not have easily available a social group of non-problem drinkers. It is especially important in these cases to begin to meet new people to include in the social network. The ability to engage comfortably in conversations is necessary for this purpose.

Skill guidelines

As part of SBNT you can encourage the focal client to consider places where new people could be met. Make a list and then select a situation from the list in which to try and meet people. How to develop conversation skills is thoroughly discussed by Monti et al. (2002) as part of their coping skills training guide for people with alcohol problems. They argue that some people have misperceptions that can be obstacles to starting conversation. Here are three common misunderstandings discussed by Monti et al. (2002):

- That you should only talk about important and weighty matters. Actually, it is not necessary to start a conversation by talking about world famine or national politics. Small talk is all right. Choose something to start a conversation that the other person can easily respond to, e.g. the weather, sport.
- That it is solely your responsibility to keep up the flow of the conversation. Conversation is a two-way process, with both parties contributing in equal parts.
- That you should never talk about yourself. It is sometimes perceived that talking about ourselves is not appropriate is social situations. However, social psychology research has shown that people like others who self-disclose. Start sharing your likes and dislikes, set the example.

Here are some specific suggestions that may make starting a conversation easier (Monti et al. 2002):

⦿ Make sure that you are attentive and observe others. You will be able to hear what people talk about to others and discover their interests, e.g. football or cooking.
⦿ You can then ask a specific question, e.g. 'I hear that you like cooking, what are your favourite recipes?' Make good eye contact and listen attentively.
⦿ Avoid closed questions, e.g. 'Was the book interesting?' Use instead open questions, e.g. 'What did you think about the book?' Open questions invite people to elaborate on the topic under discussion and keep the conversation flowing naturally.

Skill rehearsal

Therapists could use skill rehearsal to practise talking to a stranger sharing a seat on a bus. These two people frequently catch the same bus in the morning on the way to work, but they have never talked together before. Within this scenario, therapists should demonstrate the skills described above, and show how the use of them might lead to making a new acquaintance.

RECEIVING CRITICISM

Critical statements are often encountered in everyday life and are highly likely to occur when drinking has strained relationships with people close to us. One of the most difficult things to do in our interactions with people is to receive criticism gracefully. This may be particularly relevant when re-establishing relationships that have been affected by the drinking behaviour.

Criticism, if given and received appropriately, provides us with a valuable chance to learn things about ourselves and about how we affect other people. Interpersonal conflicts and the resulting anger or other negative feelings can interfere with our ability to build a positive support network for change.

In some cases, prior to the focal person attempting to approach someone, he/she will need to be prepared to deal with criticism and minimise conflict, and the work outlined below will help in achieving this aim.

Skill guidelines

Monti et al. (2002) have highlighted important issues to consider when responding to criticism. They argue that the main goal of receiving destructive or constructive criticism is to prevent escalation into an argument or fight. Below are some strategies that can be used when responding to criticism that may arise in the context of SBNT not only between the focal clients and network members but also between network members.

- *Pause before you respond and do not counterattack with further criticism.* If you respond with further criticism the chances are that an argument will develop and escalate.
- *Be curious about the content of the criticism.* Try to understand precisely what the person means. Ask questions, e.g. 'I am trying to understand what is it about what I said that upset you. Could you tell me more?'
- *Look for a win-win solution.* Try to find a compromise that helps both parties.
- *If the criticism is unjustified, you can reject it provided it is done in an appropriate way.* In these situations, it is important to reject the criticism politely but firmly.

Skill rehearsal

Give focal clients and network members an opportunity to practise responding to both constructive and destructive criticism. If this has been identified as a necessary area for work, scenes should be identified involving topics that the focal client anticipates being criticised for in the near future when approaching or re-establishing contact with a potential network member for example. Skill practice could be used. Therapists should elicit sufficient description of the 'criticism' being portrayed and its delivery, so that the scene is relevant to the focal client. This work should always be conducted in relation to potential or engaged network members.

Case example: Nita and her mother

During her treatment, Nita identified some difficulties in her relationship with her mother. Nita felt criticised by her mother for what had occurred at the time when she was drinking heavily. This also made it difficult for Nita to feel able to invite her mother to the sessions or even ask her for support in her efforts to change. Once identified, both the therapist and Nita worked on a plan to deal more effectively with the perceived criticisms.

Nita observed that she tended to become very defensive when meeting her mother and this would normally lead to arguments. Useful skills were discussed with Nita and she prepared a plan which she practised using skill rehearsal. The first step in that plan was not to become defensive by reminding herself of the work that she conducted in the session. It was agreed that Nita would then talk to her mother and state the following:

'I know that things have been difficult between us and that part of this is related to my past heavy drinking (finding something to agree with in the criticism). I am not clear, however, as to why you continue to look unhappy when I come to see you and I would appreciate it if you could tell me what it is (sincerely question the other person in order to clarify the criticism). I really value our relationship and would be very pleased if we can find a way of talking about the efforts to change that I am making. I would also be very pleased if you could come to one of the meetings I have with my therapist as I really value your support.' (Proposing a compromise and making a request.)

Nita prepared herself and practised this interaction through skill rehearsal with her therapist both as herself and taking the role of her mother. This gave her more confidence to respond to her situation and indeed attempt to engage her mother in the treatment sessions.

TALKING ABOUT FEELINGS AND LISTENING SKILLS

Although many people have difficulty expressing their feelings and/or listening attentively to others' feelings, both of these are communication skills that can be improved with practice. The ability to talk about feelings is particularly relevant for SBNT as a range of feelings are likely to emerge when approaching potential network members. Monti et al. (2002) discuss this area as part of their coping skills training programme for alcohol dependence.

Skill guidelines

⊙ *You can talk about your feelings.* We all have feelings and while you may not wish to disclose your innermost feelings with everybody, you can describe positive and negative experiences and feelings you have had.
⊙ *Try to share both positive and negative feelings.* Try to share a range of your feelings rather than only one kind.

Skill rehearsal

You should help the focal person identify a situation which is personally relevant, which involves approaching a potential network member and in which the focal person has had or anticipates having difficulty expressing feelings. Make sure that the client practising 'talking about feelings' is talking about his/her own feelings. A common scenario involves expressing the feeling that the focal person would like the potential network member to become involved in his/her treatment, or would simply like to add the person to his/her social support network.

Many of our clients have brought up feelings related to the loss of trust they experienced with significant others over the course of their drinking years and the impact that this has upon contact with important people. Those who have tried the techniques outlined in this session before, sometimes complain that the techniques simply do not work for them. We have found that a discussion regarding the building or rebuilding of relationships is helpful. Emphasise the point that it takes time and effort to communicate feelings effectively, especially when there is a history of broken promises. No single encounter should be expected to change things dramatically. Clients may initially be disappointed at their lack of progress because of the scepticism of others. They should be encouraged not to give up or become bitter, but to persist until, little by little, trust is rebuilt.

WORKING WITH THE FOCAL PERSON AND THE NETWORK TOGETHER

In cases where there is a social network present, both the focal person and the network should understand the different components of positive communication. If necessary, group members should be able to role play aspects of positive communication that they have previously found difficult.

Your aim is that the focal person and the network members communicate in ways which are effective and that the focal person and the network members work together to support the client's moderation or abstinence from drinking. In addition, communication skills are important because positive communication can reduce conflict and division between everyone attending the session. This should result in the client and the network working together more constructively and in a more unified manner.

Content

When someone develops a problem with drinking, that person and the people around him or her will often become stressed. The stress that is experienced can be caused by a number of different factors, one of which is poor communication. If communication is poor, this can often lead to conflict and arguments. Communication can break down for a range of reasons. Poor listening, a failure to take some responsibility for the situation or excessive blame can all contribute to communication break-down and conflict. On the positive side, however, all these communication problems can be addressed and improved and as a therapist you may be able to help the focal client and network members to identify and deal with these problems.

You can encourage the network to give examples of poor communication and what the consequences were for them. If necessary, and material has been generated, you can bring examples from previous sessions.

Skill guidelines

There are a number of basic components of good communication skills and Meyers and Smith (1995) as part of the Community Reinforcement Approach propose ways in which effective communication can be achieved. These include:

- presenting only one issue at a time
- defining the issue that you want to talk about clearly and specifically
- speaking in a way that is positive and avoids blaming the other person or people
- accepting partial responsibility for the situation and not seeing the other person as being totally at fault
- making an offer to help in the situation that you are talking about.

You can ask people to think about times when they have presented more than one issue at a time. Get the network members to generate their own examples. Use examples generated by the network that involve presenting more than one issue at a time, e.g. 'All you do is spend our money getting drunk, while you could be trying to get a job'. You can work on each example with the network members. In this case, the first task is to identify the different issues included in each statement:

- I am concerned about our finances and you spending our money.
- I am concerned about the amount of alcohol that you are drinking.
- I think that you should be trying to find a job.

You can then ask the group to suggest how to communicate the above issues one at a time and what exactly they would say. After this you move on to the second item.

Work down the list and at each stage ask the focal person and network members to generate their own examples. Where necessary, skill rehearsal can be set up to practise different ways of communicating.

Case example: Matthew and Louise

During an argument, Louise (network member) told Matthew (focal person): 'You are a total failure and a hopeless drunk.' In this example, Louise was presenting a very global criticism which included almost every component of poor communication. The first task was to explore how the example related to the components outlined before. Louise was presenting more than one issue at a time. The first issue related to Matthew's performance and the second to his drinking behaviour. Even though these two may be related to some extent, the way in which they were expressed set the scene for a possible argument and conflict. In addition to the fact that more than one issue was expressed, the criticism was not defined clearly and specifically and it was expressed in very negative terms.

In this example the therapist tried to tease out what were the issues involved in what Louise was trying to communicate. The following interaction illustrates how the therapist attempted to work with Louise.

Therapist: It sounds like you were feeling frustrated partly with Matthew's performance and partly with his drinking. Rather than expressing all these issues together, it might help Matthew to know more precisely what you are trying to communicate. If we take the first issue, perhaps you can think about what you mean specifically when you state that Matthew is a total failure.

Louise: I think that I said it in a moment of extreme anger. Deep down I know that he is not a total failure, but I am very frustrated at the way in which his work appears to have deteriorated since he started drinking so heavily. Also at home, he has become extremely unreliable and I cannot count on him to do anything any longer.

Therapist: I can understand your frustration and worry. Once again, it seems that there are at least two issues that you are concerned about. The first one is his performance at work and the second one his ability to help in the house. We can take the first issue further in order to practise communication skills. Perhaps you can tell us more specifically what are your concerns about his job performance.

Louise: If I am honest I feel terrified that if the situation does not change, he might lose his job and we will be in extreme financial difficulties. I think that the problem is his drinking. If he continues to drink before and during work, they will soon find out and give him the sack.

Therapist: Perhaps we can think about some of the points that we were discussing earlier in the session about speaking in a way that is positive and offering help in the situation. Could you think of any ways in which you could help?

Louise: I could perhaps talk to him in the morning about how he is feeling and review the positive reasons for changing the drinking so that the benefits of not drinking are very clear in his mind at the time when he might be feeling more vulnerable and tempted to have a drink.

Therapist: That sounds like a good idea. Perhaps we can think next about how to communicate all this to Matthew, bearing in mind the points that we discussed. How about saying something like: 'I feel very worried and concerned about the possibility of you losing your job because of your drinking. I think that if that were to happen we will all suffer and I would like to help in any way I can. I thought that it might be helpful if we talked about how you feel and the positive reasons for changing your drinking early before you go into work, and this might help you to resist the temptation or urge to drink, but I need you to tell me whether this would be helpful.'

Louise: That sounds fine, but I am not sure I can remember it.

Therapist: Well, the next step is to try it out by saying it to Matthew directly. We can practise here so you can experience what it feels like to communicate these feelings.

Skill rehearsal

The therapist can then arrange a skill rehearsal to provide the opportunity for practice and learning of the skills. A further problem with communication is that a number of barriers can prevent good communication. You can discuss this and ask people to generate examples of these barriers such as anger, lack of trust, fear. You can then go on to discuss how these barriers could be minimised or overcome.

Some time should be devoted to a discussion about how to increase positive communication between all those present. Where appropriate common failures of communication could be covered.

You can make clear that we all make some common mistakes but relationships can be improved if these negative habits can be replaced by more positive approaches.

⊙ *Kitchen sinking*: it is easy to bring in everything but the kitchen sink when involved in an argument. 'You always criticise me – last week in front of my parents, two years ago at your birthday party in front of our guests, even the day we met you told me off for folding bits of paper when I should have been listening to your words of wisdom'. If this is discussed and examples considered then it is possible to focus an argument on just the here and now.

⊙ *Mind-reading*: instead of jumping to conclusions it is wise to listen and clearly understand what is being said. 'Your mother needs help' could be interpreted in many ways, e.g. 'Your mother is a pain' or 'Your mother is frail and needs help with her housework' or 'Your mother needs help setting up the TV that we bought her'. It is easy during a bad day to mind-read and get the wrong end of the stick.

⊙ *Heel digging*: being obstinate, refusing to change even against the evidence. This can hinder any attempt to change a relationship or even develop a treatment plan. Looking for win-win solutions or trying an experiment for a few weeks are two ways of counteracting heel digging.

Usually these ways of reacting can be discussed with a sense of humour especially if the therapist and network members can provide examples.

Homework exercise

Ask those present to practise the skills developed during the week and to report at the next session how they have used the communication skills during the week.

WORKING UNILATERALLY WITH NETWORK MEMBERS

In a situation where you may have been working with the focal client and network, and the focal client stops attending the sessions, communication becomes very important. In our experience, a number of key questions emerge for network members. How can we approach Sonia after she started drinking again? What can we say? Are going to make things worse?

As a therapist you can provide an opportunity for the network members to discuss strategies to respond to this situation. Use some of the strategies and concepts covered in the previous section in order to discuss ways of communicating concern that are supportive and not critical.

Case example: Carla, Lloyd and Sonia

Carla had made good progress with her drinking and invited her parents Lloyd and Sonia for the second session during which a number of issues were discussed including information about drinking problems. At the time of the third session, only Lloyd and Sonia arrived. The therapist enquired about the situation and both Lloyd and Sonia said that they were rather concerned and thought that Carla was having some difficulty maintaining her treatment gains and was becoming distant. The therapist discussed with them possible ways of approaching the subject. They decided that there were two things they wanted to communicate to her. First, the fact that they were worried about her. Second they wanted to invite her back to continue with the sessions. Lloyd agreed that he would contact Carla and asked how she was doing. He would call her on her mobile. He would then state very clearly that both he and Sonia were worried about how she was and both wanted to continue to support her efforts to change. He would then suggest that it would be helpful for all to come back to the next session with the therapist so that they could continue the positive work. The therapist suggested using skill rehearsal to give Lloyd a chance to practise the actual skills and experience the situation before approaching Carla. This was very useful and gave Lloyd and Sonia an opportunity to discuss their concerns about how she may react and identify positive ways of communicating with her.

CORE TOPIC: COPING

RATIONALE

Looking at the individual in context involves an understanding of the interactions between the focal person and those close to him/her. The ability of a social network to offer positive support to the focal person will depend to a large extent upon the way in which the different network members are responding to the drinking behaviour and the ways in which the focal person is affected by these responses. An understanding of the different ways of responding which we call 'coping' is important for this task. As a therapist you need to be familiar with the concepts outlined in the remainder of this section.

The material covered in this section can be used in three ways. It can be used as part of work with the focal person in order to engage potential network members; it can be used when both the focal person and the network are together; or it can be used with the network members unilaterally in order to re-engage the focal person in treatment. How specifically this is done is discussed in more detail below.

When faced with alcohol problems, relatives and others concerned about the problem drinker attempt to respond to the situation. They usually try different strategies depending for example on their personalities, their previous experience, the severity of the problem. A potential difficulty is that it is often the case that a number of people are in possession of only partial information and have not combined forces effectively to understand and respond effectively to the problem. This can be addressed as part of the work in this core session.

The network members' responses to the drinking behaviour, which we call 'coping', are broader than just actions. Actions are usually accompanied, and indeed influenced, by attitudes and feelings.

In our work, we have found that the full range of possible coping strategies were evident in network responses prior to treatment and that there were numerous examples of inconsistencies in the responses by different members of a network. It was often the case that within the same household family members responded differently to the drinking. Sons and daughters, specially those of school age, were more likely to use withdrawal and avoidance (further details about these different ways of coping are given later in the section) whereas spouses, partners and parents used tolerant or controlling strategies. Family members not living in the household were more likely to withdraw but were not always consistent.

Different ways of coping lead to different results, both for the network member and for the problem drinker. The fact that results are varied is one reason why people find it difficult to decide on the best course of action, and their attempts to make these decisions are experienced as dilemmas.

Research has supported the idea that network members coping efforts fall into three broad categories. These have been called *engaged*, *tolerant* and *withdrawal* coping. Each one of these will be described in more detail.

Engaged coping

This category includes those responses which involve active attempts by the network member to change the problem drinker's behaviour. In some cases this may include attempts to *control* drinking, e.g. encouraging the problem drinker to promise not to drink, or trying to control his or her money in some way; in other cases the network member may express strong *emotions* on account of the alcohol use, e.g. starting an argument about the drinking, or making threats that the network member does not mean to carry out; yet in some instances the communication may be more *assertive* and involve expressing in a calm and open way feelings about the problem drinker's alcohol use.

Being a broad category, a range of possible thoughts may be involved. At the more emotional end it includes thoughts such as, 'It is not fair on me', whereas in its more controlling form it is associated with thoughts such as, 'There must be something I can do'. The core aspect of this category is the active attempt by the network member driven by a desire to resolve the problem of excessive alcohol use.

The following are two examples of engaged coping:

We have made it plain to him that it upsets us when we see him in a state and we have told him that we don't want him coming to us drunk. This seems to have had some benefit.

(Father of a man with a drink problem)

My tactics and strategies to help control the problem include throwing drink away whenever I find it, I see it as an evil poison in the house. I also try to reduce her opportunities to drink.

(Husband of a woman with a drink problem)

Tolerant coping

This category includes actions that protect problem drinkers from the negative consequences of their drinking. It also includes actions such as joining the person in drinking. This form of coping is usually associated with feelings of worry and guilt. The network member might be using this way of responding to his/her predicament as a result of thoughts such as, 'Other people do not understand him/her', 'It may be my fault that he/she is drinking' and/or 'I would rather have him/her as an addict than not have him/her at all'. Underlying these coping responses, there may be a strong sense of powerlessness over the situation. The main contrast with the engaged coping described previously is that this way of coping is not a direct attempt to change the alcohol use.

The following are two examples of tolerant coping:

Even as far back as ten years ago I was aware of his drinking because I used to find small bottles. I used to turn a blind eye to it for a long time because I did not want to think that there was a problem. He always drinks at home, always alone or in my presence. . . . I supply him with a whisky which I buy from the supermarket. I change where I buy it from each day so that people don't recognise me. I am too soft towards him and always give in to him. If I did not give in to him and buy him the alcohol, life would be impossible. I am part of the problem because I always buy the alcohol for him.
(Female partner of a man with a drink problem)

Sometimes I have not interfered with her drinking as I knew she'd be asleep in half an hour.
(Male partner of a woman with a drink problem)

Withdrawal coping

This category includes actions which aim to put physical or psychological distance between the network member and the problem drinker. Attempts to distance oneself from the problem or to gain some independence can arise for two main reasons. First, a network member may feel a sense of resignation to the problem associated with thoughts such as 'the less time we spend together the better', and with emotions such as sadness, bitterness or feelings of hurt. Another set of reasons might include the desire by a network member to look after her/his own needs. This may be associated with thoughts such as 'I've got my own life to lead' and/or 'I can't help him/her if I go under too'. The emotions in this case tend to be related to self-reliance.

Withdrawal coping contrasts with both engaged and tolerant coping in a number of ways. It does not involve attempts to change the drinking in the same way that the engaged coping actions attempt to. In contrast to tolerant coping, these actions do not involve protecting the problem drinker from the negative consequences of the drinking or joining in with the user of alcohol. The core aspect of this way of coping is the distancing, mental or physical, between the network member and the problem drinker. Note that in cases where a potential network member has taken this approach the focal person may experience difficulties engaging this person as part of his/her network, particularly if the concerned and affected other is unaware of the focal person's efforts to change.

The following are two examples of withdrawal coping:

I have tried to keep up my interests as much as possible. I enjoy walking the dog, and in general I have changed my mind about the nature of happiness. I now accept happiness whenever it comes, even small moments of happiness rather than seeing it as a long term thing. I sometimes buy clothes to cheer myself up or go to the theatre.

(Mother of a man with a drink problem)

Despite there being nobody fully aware of the problem I find it useful to sometimes get away for a while. I will sometimes spend a week at my mother's or go to a friend's although I have never stayed the night at a friend's house.

(Female partner of a man with a drink problem)

Looking at the whole area of coping in a rather simplified way, one can see that the network member is faced with three options: actively to attempt to change the focal person's drinking behaviour, to let alcohol use continue and at times even join in with it, or to distance oneself from the whole situation. Of course, simplifying the picture to this extent, hides some of the difficulties and complexities associated with living close to alcohol problems and ignores the dilemmas that network members experience on a day-to-day basis. Some of these dilemmas result from the fact that both positive and negative outcomes can result from the same ways of coping. This generates a state of ambivalence and uncertainty in the network members as to which way to follow. It also ignores the fact that these types of coping do not always present in pure form and that on occasions there appears to be overlap between the different categories. It

Table 6 Three ways of coping

	Engaged	Tolerant	Withdrawal
Description	Active interaction between the network member and the problem drinker focused on attempting to change the drinking	Sometimes involve interactions, sometimes lack of action. The main result is that it removes negative consequences for the focal person	Attempts to put distance between the network member and the focal person. Sometimes driven by uncertainty sometimes by a need to look after self
Thoughts	'I ought to be able to change him/her'	'Others do not understand him/her'	'The less we are together the better'
Emotions	Angry, hurt, responsible	Powerless, guilty	Self-reliant or hurt
Actions (examples)	'Watched his/her every move or checked up on him/her, or kept a close eye on him/her'	'Given him money even when you thought it would be spent on drink'	'Avoided him/her as much as possible because of his/her drinking'
Possible advantage	May help network members to feel that they are doing something positive	Conflict may be avoided	May prevent network members becoming over involved
Possible disadvantage	It may be very stressful and make the focal person feel resentful	Network members may feel they are being taken advantage of	Network members may feel that they are rejecting and/or excluding the focal person

Source: adapted with permission from Copello, A., Orford, J., Velleman, R., Templeton, L. and Krishnan, A. (2000). Methods for reducing alcohol and drug related family harm in non-specialist settings. *Journal of Mental Health*, 9: 329–343.

is often very difficult for network members to know, for example, where independence may become rejection, or attempts to support the drinker become over-tolerant.

Table 6 summarises some of the main characteristics of the three ways of coping and can assist you in exploring this material during the meetings. The table summarises some key aspects of each of the three ways of coping, illustrating examples of thoughts and associated emotions and provides an example of a possible advantage and disadvantage of each as perceived by the network member.

Understanding this model of coping will help you as a therapist when attempting to work with focal clients and their networks.

WORKING UNILATERALLY TO ENGAGE POTENTIAL NETWORK MEMBERS

Understanding the ways in which network members are coping is very important in situations where the focal person has not managed to engage any network member in treatment. You should bear in mind that some of the reasons why network members are not involved may be related to the network members' ways of coping, in particular withdrawal coping as already discussed.

Explore with the focal person the concept of coping and the different ways in which people cope including engaged, tolerant and withdrawal. Use examples to clarify these definitions.

Go back to the network diagram and ask the focal person to think about each person that he/she has included in the diagram and to think about how they have been coping. Ask if coping has changed over time and what may be possible reasons for this.

In our experience sometimes someone with a drink problem may find it difficult initially to understand the idea that other people are coping with his/her drinking behaviour. This discussion can be very helpful therefore to alert the person to the fact that people around him/her can be affected by his/her drinking and experience stress as a result of this.

Focus the discussion on how things can be changed in order to engage potential network members in the treatment, e.g. if someone has distanced him/herself from the focal person explore how this can be changed so that he/she can become part of the support network for the focal person.

You need to focus the discussion on:

⊙ Who to engage.
⊙ How to approach him/her.
⊙ What it is about his/her present way of coping that needs to be acknowledged, discussed or changed.
⊙ If possible, set up a skill rehearsal exercise.

In cases where the focal person is isolated, you can focus the discussion on general ways of coping and how people's coping in response to alcohol problems may prevent them from becoming involved in the focal person's social network. You can explore what the focal person can do in order to alter this situation and engage potential network members.

WORKING WITH THE FOCAL PERSON AND THE NETWORK TOGETHER

Much of the self-help literature on coping contains assumptions about rights and wrongs of different ways of coping. Whereas some of these ideas might be helpful in certain cases, overall these approaches ignore the complexities of each particular situation. When using the material with the network, your task therefore is not to direct people towards a particular way of coping, but to discuss the advantages and disadvantages of current and past ways of coping, to raise awareness of alternative ways of coping and possible advantages and disadvantages of these. Each case including a focal person and their social network is unique. The goal is to raise awareness in the social network leading onto further discussion and the agreement of a strategy or policy for helping the problem drinker in his or her efforts to change.

One point to bear in mind, however, is that evidence suggests that certain forms of tolerant coping (i.e. self-sacrificing) tend to be associated with worse physical and psychological symptoms for the person doing the coping, yet it can fairly quickly be modified through discussion, with a consequent reduction in the experience of stress by the network member. Self-sacrificing coping includes actions which clearly remove the consequences of the drink at the expense of the network member's well-being. Examples of these include: clearing up mess the problem drinker had made after he/she had been drinking; giving the problem drinker money even when the network member thought it would be spent on drink; and making excuses and covering up for the problem drinker, or the network member taking the blame her/himself.

Ask those present to think about ways of coping that they would like to use in the future. You should be familiar with the ways of coping covered in the previous section. Encourage those present to contrast different ways of coping and to describe in detail some of the dilemmas that they face when trying to decide a course of action. You should remain alert to thoughts, feelings and attitudes associated with different forms of coping. Table 7 illustrates a more detailed typology of coping and the different types of emotions and thoughts associated with each type.

Ask questions in order to facilitate discussion.

⊙ What happens after you become angry and start blaming X?
⊙ What do you think that you were trying to achieve when you made the rule about not drinking in the house?

Table 7 Emotions and thoughts associated with ways of coping

Action	Emotion	Thought
Control	Worried, responsible, desperate, exhausted	There must be something I can do
Tolerance	Worried, guilty, powerless	Other people do not understand him/her It may be my fault
Emotional	Angry, hurt, bewildered	It's not fair on me I blame him/her
Avoidance	Hurt, bitter, sad	We're better off apart The less time we spend together the better
Inaction	Bewildered, hopeless, indifferent	I don't know what to do I don't want to think about it
Supportive	Love for him/her, optimism	I've never given up hope for him/her
Confrontation	Strong, calm	I've got to be firm to help him/her She/he should know how I feel
Independence	Self-reliant	I've got my own life to live I can't help him/her if I go under too

Source: adapted from Orford, J., Rigby, K., Miller, T., Tod, A., Bennett, G. and Velleman, R. (1992). Ways of coping with excessive drug use in the family: a provisional typology based on the accounts of 50 close relatives. *Journal of Community and Applied Social Psychology*, 2: 163–183. Copyright © John Wiley & Sons Ltd. Reproduced with permission.

⊙ Have you noticed anyone else responding in a way that you feel is good?
⊙ Do you feel that your efforts and ways of responding are at odds with those of others?

Encourage those present to reflect upon the consequences of responses that are likely to reinforce the drinking, e.g. extreme forms of tolerance or inaction and withdrawal. You may find that for some members of the network it is easier to occupy certain positions, e.g. to be tolerant might be easier for a friend than a partner. Contrast the previous forms of coping with supportive confrontation (e.g. expressing in a calm and assertive manner the negative effect that the drinking is having upon the relationship while stating the intention to support efforts to change) and discuss the difficulties associated with these types of responses. How do you communicate the supportive aspects of this form of responding while stating clearly and firmly your position in relation to their drinking? Are there any fears associated with this type of action?

In some cases we have found that network members are worried about being too controlling or somehow impinging upon the focal person's rights to choose what he/she wants to do. This needs to be acknowledged and handled carefully. You should acknowledge this feeling while at the same time you could explore what the focal person sees as helpful for him/her in relation to network members' coping.

Reinforce the idea that the most important issue is to develop a kind of 'policy' so that efforts are coordinated and consistent. Once again, ask the client to comment from his/her experience. Explore the impact of inconsistencies, e.g. family members decide to stop serving alcohol at mealtimes but a friend invites him/her out to the pub (the usual drinking place) after the meal. Lead the discussion towards the agreement of a course of action which is consistent and unified.

The following case example illustrates the use of the coping material.

Case example: Mary, Kevin and Amanda

The fourth session was held with Mary (focal person), her partner Kevin and sister Amanda. During the previous meeting while talking about communication, it had become clear that Kevin was actively trying to control Mary's intake of alcohol by checking all the cupboards in the house to try to find and dispose of alcoholic drinks. This in turn would result in Mary feeling upset and resentful.

Having identified this form of coping, time was taken to discuss in detail the advantages and disadvantages associated with this type of action. Kevin spoke about his feelings of worry and despair. In carrying out the checks, Kevin felt that he was doing something positive and active about the problem, although he recognised that in the long run, Mary could find ways of hiding the drink from him and this would not be very helpful. Mary stated that she felt resentful about Kevin's attempts to control her drinking. The question of trust emerged and a discussion followed about how to re-establish trust in each other.

Overall it was felt that the disadvantages associated with Kevin's way of coping outweighed any possible advantage and alternatives were explored. It was agreed that as an alternative Kevin would ask Mary each day how she was feeling and how difficult it had been to avoid having a drink. Kevin would state his support by restating positively that he was prepared to support Mary in her attempts to change. Kevin felt that in this way he would feel that he was attempting to do something about the problem while avoiding the 'cat and mouse' situation that emerged in the past as a result of his controlling coping actions.

In our work we found that the most common changes in relation to coping actions by network members were:

⊙ ensuring network members took greater care of themselves
⊙ helping the focal person to avoid high risk situations
⊙ encouraging other activities

- offering telephone support
- encouraging the focal person to access other support
- setting limits such as not visiting the person if he/she had been drinking.

Coping in the face of relapse

An important issue relates to coping with relapse. Use the same model for attempting to understand what is happening in terms of network members' responses (i.e. coping) to a relapse episode. In addition to the actions, consider attitudes and feelings e.g. he/she will never make it (pessimism); he/she is hopeless (nihilism); we are wasting our time (disappointment). Challenge some of the negative thoughts and feelings and predictions of failure. Some of the more negative feelings may lead to withdrawal and distancing whereas some of the thoughts that minimise the focal person's ability to deal with the problem may lead to more engaged or controlling responses.

Attempt to reframe the relapse as an opportunity to try different ways of responding and supporting the focal person towards sustained change. Explain that relapse is common in addiction problems and attempt to develop a consistent response that acknowledges the difficulties in maintaining progress while at the same time leaving room for positive support.

The aim is for everyone to continue to work towards change and remain engaged in a supportive way. One of the advantages of a network based response is that no one needs to feel that all the responsibility for supporting the focal client rests on their shoulders alone.

WORKING UNILATERALLY WITH NETWORK MEMBERS

The coping material can be very useful in working with network members unilaterally, i.e. while the focal person is not attending the meetings. Using the model outlined in this section, you can explore different ways of coping or responding and the associated advantages and disadvantages. In addition you will need to consider the likely impact of these strategies upon re-engaging the focal person in treatment.

Bear in mind that supportive approaches from network members that are consistent are more likely to succeed in re-engaging the focal person. It could be that network members take it in turns to try to re-engage the focal person, that they pool their ideas on how to do this and vote on the best one, or that they visit the focal person in pairs to give each other support. One of the strengths of SBNT is that network members are able to support each other.

CORE TOPIC: ENHANCING SOCIAL SUPPORT

RATIONALE

Monti et al. (2002) developed the idea of enhancing support networks for people with alcohol problems as part of their coping skills training programme. Some of their ideas have informed this work. The material covered within this topic can be used with slight adaptations, either with the focal person on his/her own by focusing on building or enhancing support networks or with the focal person and any number of network members present, by focusing on widening support networks not only for the focal person but for network members as well. The overall aim guiding this work is that support can be enhanced both for the focal person and network members beyond that provided by all those present in the room.

Some of the needs for support may be already met by members of the social network present in the room. Some problem drinkers, however, may not be using network members in a way that is supportive. There is, also, an opportunity to widen the support network and also to think about those who might be supportive but have not been involved in meetings so far.

The focal person and network members (where engaged) should be able to identify people who may be supportive, neutral or not supportive, know the different types of support that are on offer and know about the different factors that make a relationship supportive, for example giving feedback and active listening. You should continue to encourage the network members and the focal client to see themselves as a team. They should see each other as a mutual source of social support.

CONTENT

You need to be familiar with and discuss the background material about social support described in this section and talk about ways in which the focal person and the network can identify who is supportive and who is not supportive.

In the long run it is possible for everyone to develop and maintain a network of people who are supportive. A supportive social network that is available will often lead people to feel more confident in managing their lives and problems. Often the emphasis in society is for people to be independent and self-sufficient yet we know that people who have a good level of social support cope better with a range of problems.

Research has shown that an individual's level of social support makes a lot of difference in their ability to cope. For example, people who go through a crisis in life such as major surgery, do better if they have the support of people around them. However, it should be remembered that supportive relationships involve a two-way experience, in order to receive support you need to offer your support to other people.

Some people in the network may think only in terms of support for solving problems but social support is useful under any circumstances and shouldn't solely be seen as a means for solving problems. It should become an integral part of life.

Part of the skill of getting and maintaining a social support network is to be able to identify people who are supportive and people who are not supportive. In order to increase the level of support encourage the focal person and network members to think about who is helpful to them. These may include the following:

⊙ Some people who are already supportive, for example family, friends, close work colleagues.
⊙ Some people who are neutral and are neither supportive nor unhelpful but have the potential to help you; for example, this may be an AA member who could be asked to be a sponsor or it may be a more distant family member.

One way of using this material is to ask the focal person and the network members to think of people they know who fit into the different categories.

⊙ *Help with solving problems*: this category includes people who may be able to help you to think about possible solutions to a problem. It may include people who have had a similar experience or faced a similar situation. For example, Ron may have had a similar problem at work and can share with you how he dealt with his problem or help you think about a possible course of action.
⊙ *Emotional support*: this includes people with whom you can talk about your feelings, both positive and negative.
⊙ *Moral support*: involves people who can give you encouragement, understanding and sometimes be close to you in difficult circumstances. For example, Mary can go to the court case to accompany Linda in order to be with her at a difficult time.
⊙ *Practical support*: includes people, who can offer very specific help with tasks, for example help with house work or decorating the flat or teaching a new skill.
⊙ *Support with information*: this may involve people who can help with information about community resources or help with looking for a job for example.
⊙ *Help in emergencies*: this may take the form of finding out about accommodation in a housing crisis or offering support with a sudden financial problem.

Case example: Margaret and Floyd

A recurring problem for Margaret had been the stress arising from her financial difficulties, which in the past had led to her drinking. While exploring social support this issue was raised by one of the network members, who felt that Margaret would benefit from some advice in relation to paying some of her bills. Her neighbour Floyd agreed to go with Margaret the following week to the Citizens' Advice Bureau, where Margaret was given guidance on managing her debts. A schedule of payments was agreed with one of the companies taking into account Margaret's income and this reduced some of the pressure considerably.

Dependable and strong relationships take time and effort to develop. The following factors should be considered when developing or enhancing a social support network (Monti et al. 2002):

- *Trying to be specific when you request help*: make it clear whether you are asking for advice or practical help with a specific task, for example: 'I would like you to come to the cinema with me next week; I would value your opinion on this situation.'
- *Adding more people to your support network*: the network of people that you have may not always meet your needs. They may not provide a type of support that would be most useful, e.g. informational or moral support. Always be open to adding more supporters to your network. It may lead to enjoyable and positive new relationships.
- *Offering support to others*: supportive relationships work both ways. As your network member may give you support, you should support him/her in return. This creates friendships that are mutually satisfying and avoids an imbalance where one person may feel overburdened or used.
- *Being positive*: always let others know what you found helpful. Be grateful and positive and let others know how they can continue to support you.

When working with the focal person on his/her own, you can use the network map to explore systematically the types and quality of support that are available to him/her. Identify any gaps and explore possibilities for change.

When working with the network, you should encourage the network to discuss the information covered. If the network does not come up with any specific problems you should ask questions to check that they have understood the information presented. The network could also be asked to use skill practice focused on ways of asking for and giving support. You could model to the network what you want them to do in the first skill practice exercise.

ENHANCING SUPPORT FOR NETWORK MEMBERS

In addition to general support you need to consider support for network members in relation to the stress arising from their situation and their attempts to respond and cope with the drink problem of the focal person. We know from what family members and others close to people with alcohol and other drug problems tell us that more often than not they feel unsupported in their coping efforts. What they say about others is in Table 8. This is particularly relevant when working with the focal person and the network. Discuss some of the sources of support failure and how they apply to those present in the room. Lead the discussion to consider possible ways of tackling some of the problems outlined in Table 8.

You need to make sure that the needs of the network members are discussed and considered, otherwise their ability to perform the required actions may be undermined.

Table 8 Why network members may feel unsupported

Barriers to accessing or receiving support
Others keep their distance and do not get involved
They live too far away
They are too busy
They encourage drinking
They disagree with how I am dealing with the problem
I feel ashamed to tell anyone
We avoid talking about it in the family
Others do not see it as a problem
We all have a different view of the problem
I always feel criticised by them

Case example: Len, his mother, Claire and Bryan

Len had been doing well in treatment and managed to maintain his abstinence from drinking. The problem however had been very severe in the recent past and his wife Claire, who had been present in the sessions, had been feeling rather isolated. When exploring the availability of social support for Claire it became clear that it was difficult for her to support Len because she herself felt very unsupported. Len's mother lived nearby but Claire felt unable to talk to her about the situation as in the past her mother had always minimised the problem. Claire feared being blamed for Len's drinking. In addition, Bryan, a friend of Len's, encouraged his drinking and

Claire found it difficult to deal with this situation which made her feel angry and upset. It was agreed that both Len and Claire would talk to Len's mother. Claire identified a friend who lived nearby and could offer moral support. Claire agreed to contact her during the next few days and some discussion took place to determine how to approach her. Claire felt that she would then be more able to support Len in his efforts to change.

The following quotes from the work of Ellis (1998) illustrate the benefits from increased support experienced by network members:

Before it was like being on our own . . . you get a rejected feeling . . . you're asking for help and there's none out there.

(A partner)

It was good for me because I did not feel that I had to tackle the problem on my own.

(A girlfriend)

The following case example illustrates work on widening the support network for the focal person.

Case example: Anjula, Emma and Safeena

During the course of the meeting, Anjula (focal person) and Emma (network member, a friend of Anjula) identified Safeena, a mutual friend whom Anjula had not seen for a long time. Emma felt that it would be useful for Anjula to get in touch with Safeena and arrange to go out in order to widen her social contacts. Emma thought that it was important for Anjula to develop other contacts in addition to those people involved in her treatment. Anjula agreed and a plan of action was developed which involved ringing Emma the following day and arranging to meet.

Your overall aim is that the focal client and the network should have some ideas about what they can do to help and support one another and if necessary how to widen support networks. A reminder sheet with a summary of the material is included in Appendix 8.

ALCOHOLICS ANONYMOUS AND OTHER SELF-HELP GROUPS

As already discussed, one potential way of increasing support is through self-help groups such as Alcoholics Anonymous (AA). There are increasing numbers of possible self-help groups that are available for people with alcohol and other addiction problems. Research has shown that increased participation in AA for example is associated with reductions in alcohol use.

In the context of SBNT, self-help groups can offer accessible social support, sometimes over a 24-hour period and contact with people who have had a similar experiences and can act as role models for positive change and improvement. This type of support has been particularly helpful for people who are isolated or whose contacts are mainly with others supportive of continued drinking. In addition, studies have shown that people who receive support from AA during and after treatment can achieve better outcomes. Contact with self-help can be organised during a session or used as a homework task.

CORE TOPIC: NETWORK BASED RELAPSE MANAGEMENT

RATIONALE

The goal in Social Behaviour and Network Therapy is to promote a shared understanding of the relapse process with all those present and to discuss possible strategies that will help the focal person to avoid lapse or relapse with a particular emphasis on social support and positive support for change. Hence, as a therapist you need to encourage the focal person to think about ways of using the network to support his/her attempts to avoid lapse or relapse. The work for this topic was informed by the ideas about relapse and relapse prevention originally developed by Marlatt and Gordon (1985). The work has a clear network focus.

The aim of this work is therefore on developing both an understanding of the relapse process and a plan of action to be followed in cases of both lapses and relapses. The plan should involve not only the focal client but also network members. In cases where you are working with the individual problem drinker and there are no other network members present in the meeting, you should aim to develop a relapse management plan that involves other people, e.g. a self-help group, a family member that lives at a distance, as well as the problem drinker. The emphasis should be on the role of social support in the management of lapses or relapses and therefore on the ways in which other people can support the focal person in his/her attempts to avoid future problematic alcohol use. The key skill in this type of work for you as a therapist is to *think network* as previously described in this manual.

The contents of this session are equally relevant for those working towards abstinence or moderation. The aim is to work towards and maintain the defined behavioural goal, i.e. no consumption in the case of an abstinence goal or predefined and agreed limits in the case of moderation. You should aim to progress towards the agreed goal and avoid any setback away from it which is seen as a lapse or relapse.

AIMS

You will need to familiarise those present with the concepts and ideas related to both the process of relapse and relapse prevention work and help the focal person and the network to develop a variety of skills and the confidence to avoid lapses to problem alcohol use.

You will need to ensure that both the problem drinker and network members have a set of strategies and beliefs that reduce the fear of failure and prevent lapses turning into relapses, and that they agree on a plan of action that involves a number of people and could be used in cases where either lapse or relapse have occurred.

You will need to acknowledge that temptation to drink is normal in those attempting to change behaviour and as such it is something to be discussed in the context of conducting this work. It is useful sometimes here to use the analogy of a 'fire drill' stating that even though you do not expect a fire to occur, you can still prepare yourself in case it happens.

KEY CONCEPTS

In order to conduct this work you will need to be familiar with a number of concepts. In our experience, network members are unlikely to be familiar with these concepts, mostly perceiving the alcohol problem as an all or nothing event i.e. the problem is either present or not. Part of the importance of this work in SBNT is to introduce the notion of recovery from alcohol problems as a process. This may reflect a new way of understanding the problem for those in the session. It is also important to emphasise the notion that even though people may have setbacks, these can be part of the road to recovery. Setbacks can be used as learning opportunities. It may be useful to introduce the following concepts as part of the work:

High risk situations

This term is used to define situations that both the focal person and other network members can identify as those which pose the most significant danger for the focal client who is trying to resist returning to drinking in a problematic fashion. These situations may include going to a party, meeting old drinking friends, becoming angry or upset, feeling lonely, having an argument with a network member or someone else, etc.

Lapses or slips

These terms are used to refer to a short-lived and relatively isolated return to the use of alcohol (any alcohol in the case of abstinence or amounts above the agreed limit in the case of moderation) after a period during which the goal of treatment had been successfully achieved. These terms signify a short-lived return to drinking that can be stopped quickly as opposed to a return to pre-treatment levels of full-blown problematic use over a longer period.

Relapse

Relapse is a term used for a return to constant heavy drinking or repeated episodes of heavy drinking after a period of successful achievement of the intervention goal.

CONTENT

The general rationale for preventing relapse includes the following:

- explaining that lapses or relapses can be prevented
- aiming to identify high risk situations in the future
- agreeing an overall policy to be adopted, by all network members, towards risky situations and relapse
- developing a specific plan allocating tasks and roles to all those present.

Preventing relapse needs more than just willingness to change and skills. In addition an adequate level of positive support needs to be developed in order to respond successfully to triggers and the environment that can contribute to lapses or relapses. In particular, in the context of SBNT, attention is paid to the development of positive support and support for non-drinking activities and the reduction of support for continued problematic use of alcohol.

Skill guidelines

- *Identifying high risk situations*: this work involves identifying in detail issues such as when, where, and with whom the focal person feels most vulnerable in terms of relapse. In addition, particular thoughts and feelings may also precede high risk situations. You can ask those present to think of situations which have caused difficulties in the past. Encourage those present to think of signs that in the past have proven to lead to lapses or relapse.
- *Agreeing an overall policy*: this usually follows from a shared understanding about relapse and in particular the realisation that lapses and relapses commonly occur. Foster a

positive orientation towards helping the focal person and minimise attitudes that may foster feelings of failure or being criticised on the part of the focal person.

⊙ *Developing a specific plan*: the emphasis here is on developing a relapse management plan that involves other people in the focal person's social network. Network members may be particularly good at identifying early signs of relapse and a range of responses could be explored at the meeting. Care should be taken to minimise the possibility of conflict or the focal person feeling criticised or 'got at' by other network members at times of risk. The discussion also needs to address the need for network members' mutual support when helping the focal person at times of high risk or relapse.

In cases where the focal person is isolated, the plan needs to consider contacts with outside agencies such as self-help groups or day centres. If you have been working with an isolated focal person by this stage you may have identified potential new sources of support and you can consider these in the development of a network based relapse management plan.

Case example: Tony, Catherine and Geoff

Tony had made good progress during the early part of the treatment but the risk of relapsing back into problematic drinking was acknowledged both by him and the network members, who included his wife Catherine and his brother Geoff. The therapist spent some time discussing relapse and the importance of developing strategies to deal with the triggers in the environment that can contribute to relapse. During the meetings it became clear that Friday evenings were a high risk time for Tony, as Catherine worked till late on Fridays and Tony found that being on his own at home after a hard week could sometimes make him think about how nice it would be to have a drink. Having identified Friday evening as a high risk time for relapse for Tony, a number of possible options were discussed by all present. Options such as Catherine coming home earlier were explored but seen as impractical. Finally it was agreed that Geoff would contact Tony on Fridays at 6 p.m. by telephone and check how Tony was feeling. If Tony felt at risk of relapse, they would agree to meet and do something together in the evening in order to minimise the risk of Tony being on his own and unable to resist the temptation to drink

Case example: Graham and Malcolm

Graham had considerable difficulty developing relationships and the focus of the sessions had been on creating a positive social support network. A positive outcome from the sessions had been that Graham attended a day centre where he met some people and where Graham was spending one morning every week. When exploring the area of relapse, the discussion focused on how this new developed contact could be used in helping Graham to deal with high risk situations for relapse. Graham had struck up a good supportive relationship with Malcolm, who was also attending the day centre. Graham and the therapists agreed that it would be important for Graham to be able to attend the day centre at times when he felt vulnerable but it was recognised that at present Graham did not want to attend any more days per week. Both Graham and the therapist agreed that it would be useful if Graham knew that he could attend the centre on any given day if he felt vulnerable. It was agreed that Graham would approach the person running the day centre and ask whether this could be organised. At Graham's request, the therapist also telephoned the day centre manager and this strategy was agreed by everyone concerned.

Case example: Dean and George (the publican)

Dean had a serious alcohol problem which had become worse over the past few years after his marriage broke up. Dean was rather isolated and his main social contacts revolved around the pub. Every afternoon as he arrived at the pub George, the publican, who knew Dean very well, would pour his favourite pint of strong beer as soon as Dean walked through the door. Over the months, this had become a well-established ritual. During the sessions of SBNT, Dean and his therapist identified going to the pub as a high risk situation. The problem was that going to the pub was important for Dean as it provided him with his only social contact. After some discussion during the session, the therapist arranged to go to visit George (the publican) with Dean during the next session. This took place the following week and during the meeting it was agreed that every time that Dean came to the pub, George would continue to pour a drink in a pint glass as Dean walked through the door, but instead of beer, the drink would be orange juice. This was very successfully carried out over the next few weeks. In addition, following the meeting Dean felt that he could approach George at any time and talk about some of his difficulties.

CHAPTER 6

Phase 3: Final meeting

PLANNING FOR THE FUTURE AND TERMINATION

RATIONALE

Research has shown that what happens after treatment is important in determining the maintenance of progress achieved. Your aim at the end of treatment should therefore be to create the necessary conditions for the network to continue to provide *positive support for change* or the maintenance of positive change that occurred during the intervention and hence increase the chances of long-term success.

By this stage, you would have done some work focused on relapse management. Preparation should include a revision of possible lapses and relapses and how the focal client and other network members will attempt to respond to these events. Both the focal client and all the network members should see themselves as at least partially responsible for the ongoing success of the treatment.

Everyone plays a role in helping the focal client to maintain the goal of either decreased drinking or abstinence. For the focal person to maintain the goal of decreased drinking or abstinence she/he will need the help and support of the network. For the network to support the focal person effectively members will need to help and support each other.

CONTENT

This meeting is about planning for the future and the maintenance of positive change. The focus of the treatment sessions has been to build network support that will be useful in the future. This session on planning for the future follows on from this basic philosophy. It is important for the network to be able to plan as far as it is possible for any small or large crises or significant events that may occur in due course. This should help the focal client and network to cope well in the long term.

This session is about looking into the future and anticipating what changes may happen that may risk the progress made and how to maintain the treatment gains. It is difficult to predict all possible future events but here are a few examples: death of a close family member, a child leaving home, health problems, divorce or separation, adjustments to new challenging situations, financial changes, promotion or demotion at work. Events that happen to people around you may also affect you, for example if friends react differently towards you because they are preoccupied with concerns of their own. Encourage each of those present to think of a life event or life change that he or she thinks may happen in the future.

The network should prepare a general plan about how to approach changes in their lives in the future with particular relevance to those changes that may affect the focal person. The changes may be either positive or negative but it is necessary to think of some general strategies for coping and stress the need for continued support. You should spend some time exploring in depth and if necessary challenging the network's plans and ensuring that their plans are viable and practical. This session can be very practical and active, with those present considering different scenarios and different possible responses. The orientation should involve everyone being prepared and remaining positive and hopeful about the future.

A further area to concentrate on is that of the network's response to drinking. Research has shown that support for problematic drinking is associated with poor outcomes so this needs to be considered by all those present. How can this be minimised? How are network members going to respond if this type of support becomes prominent?

Finally, in some cases where the focal person has stopped attending, you may need to address how the network will respond in the future, at a time when the focal person is more willing to consider change than at present. It is possible that by this stage of the intervention you are working with the network unilaterally. It is important for you as a therapist to communicate that change can continue to happen beyond the duration of active treatment and network members' responses to that change in the future will be important in providing support to the focal person. You need to avoid the situation where a network member feels that everything possible has been tried and nothing is ever going to work. Emphasise positive support for change, attempt to reduce punitive or blaming responses, and encourage the network to provide mutual support for each other. Promote hope and realistic optimism.

Emphasise the idea of the network continuing to meet after treatment particularly in cases where relapse occurs. The network can use the skills developed during the treatment to respond to situations which are likely to arise in the future. Emphasise the positive skills that network members have to respond to future situations.

You should end by reviewing the previous sessions and encouraging the client and the network members to continue working together and supporting each other in the future, stressing the crucial importance that natural processes play in recovery from alcohol problems. Provide plenty of positive feedback for what has been achieved.

Case example: Margaret, Lucy, Sophie, Floyd and Wilson

At the final meeting Margaret was seen at home with her friend Lucy and her neighbours Floyd and Wilson. Sophie, Margaret's sister, had attended some of the meetings but had been unable to attend the final one due to a prior personal commitment. Following a review of progress, the main part of the meeting focused on the future and how to maintain a positive support network even in the event of a lapse or relapse. First, a discussion focused on possible difficulties in the future. Margaret's brother was ill and his possible deterioration was seen as a potential problem for Margaret, who in the past had tended to respond to these situations by drinking. Margaret's tendency to 'bottle things up' was also identified as a potential high risk situation. In addition, Margaret sometimes found changes at work stressful. Each event and the possible problems arising from it were discussed at some length and possible ways in which network members could support Margaret were identified. Floyd said that he would attempt to talk to Margaret about her feelings related to her brother's illness and try to offer his support. He felt that he could do this, particularly as he had a personal experience similar to Margaret's. The therapist raised the question of possible relapse and how network members would support Margaret in this event. Each network member described how he/she would attempt to respond to this hypothetical event and finally Margaret was invited to offer her views. In general it was agreed that network members would attempt to talk to Margaret and also talk to each other for mutual support. Reminding Margaret about the progress made during treatment and the difficulties she faced while drinking heavily was seen as a useful strategy to adopt in such a situation. In addition Lucy and Margaret agreed that Margaret would continue to record her drinking in a drinking diary and that they both would review her progress every two weeks. Towards the end of the meeting the therapist summarised the progress achieved and thanked everyone for the hard work that had occurred during and between meetings.

A few months later, the therapist received a telephone call from Margaret. After a period of good progress Margaret had resumed heavy drinking. Margaret contacted Lucy who at that point met with her. Lucy encouraged

Margaret to contact other network members and offered to do this with her. They reconvened a meeting at which it was decided to reinstate the relapse management plan that helped Margaret get back on track.

PART 3

Elective topics, training and common questions

7

Elective topics

Therapists can use any of the elective topics presented in Part III. Elective topics can be used as the main component of a session. On the other hand, they may not take a full session and they may be combined with other core or elective topics in the same meeting. For example, education may provide an opportunity to explore communication about drinking and the effects of drinking with those present in the session therefore combining a core and elective topic. In the course of our work it has become evident that two of the elective sessions are used very frequently and are very popular with therapists. These include 'Basic information about alcohol' and 'Increasing pleasant and joint activities'. The information work, when conducted with focal clients and network members together, provides an opportunity to develop a common agreed understanding as a platform from which to work and address one of the more common problems: differing views and the confusion and uncertainty that usually surround the development of an alcohol problem both for the focal client and for those people concerned and affected by the focal client's drinking. The elective topic focusing on activities provides a positive way to explore alternatives to drinking and generate enhanced self-esteem and optimism.

It is important for the therapist to agree with those present which elective topic to use. The topics covered in this section include:

⊙ Basic information about alcohol
⊙ Increasing pleasant and joint activities
⊙ Employment
⊙ Active development of positive supports
⊙ Minimising support for problem drinking.

BASIC INFORMATION ABOUT ALCOHOL

The information contained in the prompt sheet in Appendix 2 can be given to clients if you consider that it would be useful and important even if you do not use this elective session. The contents outlined in the Appendix should act as a guideline. Different aspects may need to be covered at different levels of detail depending on the knowledge already possessed by those present. An important issue to consider is that different people in the room may have different views. In addition, in our experience we have found that those affected by alcohol problems, i.e. the network members may have little understanding or feel very confused about whether there is a problem and if so what is the extent of it.

Rationale

Information is important in the context of SBNT as it allows you to:

⊙ establish the level of understanding of alcohol problems of both the focal person and network members
⊙ try to reach an agreed understanding of alcohol problems.

The prompt sheet in Appendix 2 outlines some information that can be used during the session. You should have familiarised yourself with this information prior to the meeting. Note that this work will allow you to discuss in more detail if necessary the choice of drinking goal (i.e. in cases where there has not been network agreement).

Skill guidelines

In cases where the focal person has not yet managed to engage a network member, the information contained in this topic can be discussed with him/her if you have decided that this area was important. In addition, however, potential network members' understanding of alcohol problems as perceived by the focal person should be explored, and where possible options for correcting misconceptions should be discussed, particularly if they are seen to interfere with network participation, e.g. a close relative who thinks that people with alcohol problems never change and always lie may not be willing to be engaged in any form of support for the focal person.

Review one by one people included in the network diagram constructed during Phase 1 and ask the focal person to describe his/her perception of each network member's understanding of alcohol problems. Questions like the following could be used:

- How do you think that your sister understands your problem?
- Do you think that this may be a reason why she has not been in touch?
- Are there any ways in which you could help her understand more about alcohol problems?

Possible options are to approach network members, describe the current problem, attempt to change misconceptions, and state the need for support. These could be explored at this stage and set as homework tasks or conducted as part of the communications skills work. For example, referring to the previous example, the focal person can write a letter to the sister acknowledging the difficulties experienced so far by both, explaining that people with alcohol problems <u>can</u> change and that he/she is engaged in treatment actively trying to do this. A statement can follow acknowledging that re-establishing a positive relationship would be valuable.

Case example: Kim and Elspeth

Kim had a very difficult relationship with her mother Elspeth. Kim thought that her mother saw her as a total failure since Kim lost her job as a result of her heavy drinking. Kim's father had a serious alcohol problem and had died of cirrhosis of the liver. Kim's mother thought that Kim was following in his footsteps. During the meeting, Kim and her therapist tried to understand Kim's mother's position and her understanding of Kim's alcohol problem which was clearly based on her previous experience. Following the meeting, Kim contacted her mother and stated clearly that even though she had a problem with alcohol this did not mean that she could not change and that she would value her support.

In cases where network members are present, you may find that different people have different levels of understanding of the problem or indeed have their own clear ideas about its cause and required actions. You should check the network members' knowledge about alcohol and provide any information in accordance with an understanding of the problem which acknowledges the contribution of social factors in the maintenance and resolution of alcohol problems.

The discussion should then focus on attempting to define the extent of the problem with the aim of arriving at a view which is shared by the majority if not all members of the network.

You may find that problem drinkers or other members of the network have already developed ideas about 'alcoholism' or 'addiction'. Indeed in some cases, you might be asked whether in your view the problem drinker is in fact an 'alcoholic' or suffering from 'dependence'. If you are faced with these questions, you might say that this treatment aims to de-emphasise labelling or categorising people as 'sick'. You can then discuss the results of information gathered during your initial assessment, where possible relating the results to what you know about the general popu-lation, hence allowing those present to make sense of the problem. You should then attempt to redirect the discussion to the question of how the problem is affecting everyone present in the room and use this as an opportunity to continue to build support for change.

Case example: Harry, Susan and Bill

When Harry had his first meeting with other network members, it became apparent that different views about his drinking were held by different people. His father Bill thought that Harry was an 'alcoholic' and should therefore not drink at all. Harry, however, wanted to moderate his drinking and his wife Susan was rather confused as to whether Harry had a serious problem or not. During the session Harry's drinking was explored in the context of the provision of information. An agreement was reached by everyone at the end of the meeting. All agreed that Harry had a serious alcohol problem. Harry decided to stop drinking altogether for three months before considering any other drinking goal.

In this case, in addition to the provision of information, the therapist was aiming for a 'win-win' solution where different people had different views. By agreeing to stop drinking for an initial period of three months, the therapist managed to obtain a commitment from everyone in the room. Harry was prepared to try this, provided he could keep his long-term options open and he did not have to commit to being abstinent forever, something he felt was very difficult to contemplate. Both Bill and Susan were happy to agree a goal that involved abstinence.

INCREASING PLEASANT AND JOINT ACTIVITIES

Rationale

Monti et al. (2002) have developed the idea of increasing pleasant acti-vities for people with alcohol problems as part of their Coping Skills Training Programme. This topic is based on the idea that pleasant activities are important both for the focal client and also any network member present. Problem drinking may have resulted in a reduction of pleasure for everyone. Working with the focal client and the network offers an opportunity to explore and plan joint pleasurable activities. Pleasant activities are related to positive feelings and provide an alternative to drinking. In addition, pleasant activities facilitate cohesion and positive support in the long term.

It is important during this work to make sure that the activity times set are realistic and practical. If you think that the activity selected and the times required for it are not realistic, you need to discuss this.

Skill guidelines

The first step in increasing pleasant activities is to identify some possible pleasant activities that are relevant to each individual. You can ask those present to brainstorm a list of activities. Emphasise quantity at this stage and once you have a list available ask those present to think about those activities which are particularly relevant for them. Some examples of activities include going to the cinema, dancing, changing one's hairstyle, writing a letter to someone you have not seen for years, searching the web for old friends, writing a short story, going for a picnic, watching people, flying kites. The list can go on and on.

The next step, having chosen some activities which are relevant to each person, is to develop a plan. Ask those present to schedule a minimum of 30 minutes which are set aside for pleasant activities. Some activities may take a lot longer. You may find that some of the activities chosen are best carried out individually and some in a group, including the focal client and network members. You need to make sure that what is planned is realistic and therefore likely to succeed.

Explore possible strategies to increase pleasant activities and also potential obstacles. Encourage those present to think of possible obstacles and also strategies to deal with these obstacles.

Aim to have both the focal person and network members creating a list of activities that each person likes doing. In addition, encourage them to think about ways of coping with problems that may arise and that may lead to abandoning the plan.

Use some of the chosen activities to set homework tasks to be reviewed at the following meeting. Remember that positive joint activities can provide alternatives to problem drinking and enhance mutual positive support.

Case example: Fred, Alice and Toby

Fred had attended a number of sessions of SBNT particularly focusing on the core topics. During the early part of treatment it was noted that Fred and his partner Alice were spending little time on pleasant activities, since most of the time they were dealing with the problems caused by Fred's drinking. Fred had made some good progress and it was now time to fill his new spare time with pleasant alternative activities to drinking. Toby, a friend of Fred, was invited to this meeting and this was seen as an opportunity to explore ways of increasing pleasant activities. The therapist asked everyone to brainstorm ideas about different activities relevant to each one of them and for them as a group. The therapist had to prompt them by suggesting examples such as going to the theatre, watching a football match or going for a picnic at the weekend. This helped everyone to think about options. The discussion went on to focus on how realistic these activities were at this point.

All those present liked the suggestion of a picnic, given that the weather was pleasant at that time of the year. Their attention turned to how to organise this and explore any possible obstacles that might get in their way. Toby said that he knew of a good place and suggested that they went on a particular date in two weeks' time. Alice and Fred agreed to organise all the food and this would also allow them to carry out some activity together which up to the point of coming to treatment they had not been doing very often. The discussion then turned to possible problems that might interfere with the plan. Toby stated that he had a very busy schedule over the next month but he would make sure that that time was set aside for this activity. Fred talked about his tendency to pull out of things at the last minute and it was agreed that Alice would keep reminding him of the importance of making sure that this plan was carried out.

The therapist finished the session on a positive note reinforcing the work all present were doing.

EMPLOYMENT

Rationale

In the context of SBNT assisting a focal person to seek employment may have an important role in helping to develop wider social contacts through meaningful occupations which in turn may lead to the ultimate goal of treatment: achieving a 'positive supportive social network for change'.

This area of work is important for people who are out of work and need to return to some form of employment or those who work in an environment which supports continued problem drinking and need to consider a change. If necessary you can use some of the materials included in the elective topic, minimising support for problem drinking, in order to deal with this situation. The point of covering this topic is to consider the person's social environment and the development of positive support, as opposed to just job seeking.

Skill guidelines

There are a number of steps involved in obtaining meaningful work. The tasks necessary to achieve this involve:

- ⊙ reviewing past work experience including strengths and weaknesses
- ⊙ selecting the area of work and exploring the current state of the job market
- ⊙ developing a plan of action including contacting people, producing a CV
- ⊙ completing application forms
- ⊙ practising interview skills.

As in previous topics, there are two possible scenarios that you may come across. In cases where network members are involved in the treatment, having identified a need to work in this area, you will need to use the time to discuss the different stages and tasks involved and encourage everyone in the network to think about a job seeking plan to support the focal person. The important aspect here is for you as a therapist to facilitate a process whereby the whole network becomes actively involved in this task as opposed to working directly with the focal person as you may do in an individualised treatment. Your role here is clearly one of being a facilitator.

In cases where the focal person is isolated and a job is seen as a way of enhancing his/her social support network, you will need to discuss the different tasks involved and help the focal person to develop a plan of action. Note that you will not have time to carry out all of the tasks outlined above. There are agencies however that can assist the focal person and your role is to help him/her to contact these agencies. Note that you will need to be familiar with the agencies available in your area. Sometimes this may involve making telephone calls or visiting an agency with the focal person. You can set some of these tasks as homework.

Case example: Monica

Monica had been out of work for some time and felt that she was losing all her confidence. In addition, her main social contact was her partner, who had some difficulties himself with alcohol and gambling. It was agreed that it would be important to think about work even though Monica felt very apprehensive about this. First it was agreed that voluntary work would constitute a good way back into some form of employment. After some skill rehearsal Monica made contact with her local voluntary bureau and organised an interview. After a few weeks, Monica started to do some voluntary work and felt that her confidence was increasing.

ACTIVE DEVELOPMENT OF POSITIVE SUPPORTS

Rationale

The material in this section is particularly suitable for people who are isolated and for whom additional work is needed to develop a positive support network.

Skill guidelines

In some cases, your approach may need to be more active than usual, helping the focal person to initiate a link to a resource, organisation or person who can, in the long run, become a source of positive support. For this you need to be familiar with the local community resources.

Start by reviewing who in the past has been supportive. Make sure that you have some common agreement about what is meant by positive support. Explore the ways in which the focal person experiences the identified people as supportive.

Review other potential sources of support systematically. These include, for example, other family members including the extended family, the church, colleagues from work, old friends, organisations that offer befriending, voluntary work agencies.

Identify through a discussion with the focal person the most realistic place or organisation where new contacts could be made. Introduce the concept of meeting new people if you have not done so and identify any problems that the focal person anticipates with this.

Decide on a goal that involves making contact with a new person. Ask the focal person to describe any problems and use problem-solving techniques (Goldfried and D'Zurrilla 1969) to develop strategies to deal with these problems.

Six-step problem solving

1 Identify the problem and define it as specifically as you can
2 Consider various ways of attempting to solve the problem
3 Weigh up pros and cons of each possible solution
4 Select the approach that seems most promising
5 Try it out
6 Evaluate how successful the approach has been.

In cases where this is possible and following skill rehearsal if necessary, ask the focal person to make an initial telephone call during your meeting. Make sure that you offer practice beforehand and support him/her while carrying out this task.

In other cases it might be possible to organise the next meeting so that you can accompany the person to the point of making the first contact with an organisation.

Finally, set up a homework task that involves some level of achievement of the identified goal. Make sure that the homework task is realistic and achievable and agree to review progress at the next meeting.

Case example: Jack

After a few sessions, it was still difficult to generate support for Jack. The therapist decided that perhaps he needed to be more active in supporting Jack in making some link to a community resource. A day service was identified in town where people who had had alcohol problems met. The therapist made a telephone call during the meeting to find out details such as opening hours and who could attend. The following session, the therapist and Jack met outside the centre and then spent time together at the centre so that Jack had an opportunity to make a link to the resource with support from the therapist.

MINIMISING SUPPORT FOR PROBLEM DRINKING

Rationale

This work is particularly suitable for those clients who have many people in their social network who are supportive of problem drinking. Note that it is best not to embark on this topic early in treatment; it is best addressed once core topics have been covered. The rationale for this has already been discussed; it involves the need to build up positive networks or at least increase the chances of building positive support before reducing support for problem drinking.

Skill guidelines

The first step in reducing this type of support for the focal client is to identify clearly where it is coming from. Use the network diagram to review those people in the social network who are identified as supporting problem drinking. Also consider those people with whom the focal person has got a very difficult relationship and hence contact with these people leaves him/her vulnerable to relapse.

Encourage the focal person and other network members present to think of reasons for stopping contact with people who are supporting problem drinking. Discuss the advantages and disadvantages of doing this.

In some cases it will not be possible to stop contact and you should encourage those present to think about how best to respond to situations where avoidance is not possible.

Set specific tasks as homework.

Case example: Ian, his neighbours and Cathy

Ian had few contacts apart from his neighbours, all heavy drinkers. This posed a serious problem for Ian, who periodically returned to heavy alcohol consumption, usually triggered by a visit from one of his neighbours. The therapist felt that it was important to focus on minimising the support for drinking in Ian's environment. The therapist and Ian spent some time reviewing this network of people. Ian found it difficult to say 'no' assertively to them when they came to visit, so skill rehearsal was used during the session. Finally, Ian identified Cathy, at the place where he did voluntary work, whom he got on well with and who did not drink. At the same time as minimising his contact with his neighbours, plans were made to spend more time with other people, including Cathy.

Training and common questions

SELECTION, TRAINING AND ASSESSMENT

The study protocol for training all therapists in the UK Alcohol Treatment Trial is described under the headings of selection, training, assessment and supervised practice with a rationale given for the method we used at each stage. The training approach can be adapted to various settings, intra agency and cross agency training needs. It has been further developed to be delivered as a thirty credit undergraduate module at the University of Leeds. Since the completion of UKATT, we have also delivered training to agencies where we have used the main components and ideas of SBNT in a flexible way in order to increase and promote family and network focused practice. An example of the latter work can be seen in Orford et al. (2009).

As part of UKATT the following methods were used: selection, training and assessment.

Selection

Candidates wishing to be trained to participate in the UKATT were required to submit a curriculum vitae (CV) and a short video recording of practice demonstrating ability to address more than one person in a therapeutic session. The CV was required to document two years' practice with addiction clients as basic knowledge and experience was necessary for the acquisition of SBNT skills in the time allowed. The recording of practice was required in order to demonstrate basic skills and willingness to record sessions.

Training and assessment

Training was divided into two sections: attendance at a centre for group based acquisition of knowledge and skills followed by individual supervision of recorded *in vivo* practice in at least two training cases (Tober et al. 2005). The rationale for initial group training is the provision of opportunities to develop practice by skill rehearsal with other participants. Skill acquisition is facilitated both through rehearsal and through the opportunity to be on the receiving end, to experience SBNT from the perspective of each of the focal person and network members. SBNT is a treatment which requires knowledge of resources and resourcefulness in mobilising the network to make use of these. In SBNT training, the multidisciplinary, multi-agency group brought a plethora of diverse ideas which provided inspiration for its members. Sessions were role played, ideas were shared and the experience was fun as well as being serious. Training in SBNT was a very active process where trainees engaged fully with the ideas and concepts and were eager to try out different ways of responding to situations that they faced in their day-to day-practice, particularly when encouraged to 'think network'.

The evidence then tells us that newly acquired skills need to be implemented in the real life situation, practised and subjected to monitoring and feedback if they are to be retained (Miller and Mount 2001). Once initial group training was complete, participants returned to the workplace and commenced practice with their clients. This practice was recorded and a recording provided to the practice supervisor. Individual supervision took place on a face-to-face basis or by telephone; either way it was based upon simultaneous viewing of the session for feedback and discussion. The point of this method of supervision, by no means unique to SBNT, is that it has been found to be an efficient learning tool. It avoids problems of recall and inexact reporting of the content of sessions and enables the participant to scrutinise their own practice in a safe environment.

To be deemed competent to practise, participants were required to demonstrate their knowledge and skills with two cases. The requirement for there to be eight complete sessions was relaxed, and it was deemed sufficient to show proficiency in a number of sessions with two separate cases. The UKATT training group consisted of people from different educational and training backgrounds, different professional groups, gender and age. SBNT was widely thought to be consistent with the practice of those in a range of discipline groups, namely psychiatric nursing, social work, medical, psychology, occupational therapy and counselling.

The criteria set out below were used for the assessment of competence (on a tick list basis) and for subsequent supervision sessions, designed to improve the quality of practice and to maintain therapist adherence with the treatment protocol. The criteria are based upon the content of SBNT sessions as described in this book. They are set out as a check list which can be used for training and supervision.

General criteria for all sessions

Skills

Establishing rapport
Demonstrating competence
Being authoritative
Being enthusiastic
Communicating realistic optimism
Using opportunities
Being attentive
Showing control of the session
Using positive non-verbal body language including facial expressions

Manual adherence

Structuring the sessions
Greeting the client(s)
Explaining the intervention
Defining the purpose of the session
Agenda setting
Time keeping
Maintaining focus

Things to be avoided

Confronting, challenging, sarcasm, incredulity, over-identification, giving unsolicited advice, being distracted, mirroring.

PHASE 1: IDENTIFYING THE SOCIAL NETWORK

The first meeting: setting the scene

1 Welcome those attending
2 Review pre-session change as appropriate
3 Communicate the philosophy of the treatment
4 Communicate the format of future sessions
5 Discuss, if necessary, the drinking goal
6 As appropriate, discuss the drinking goal with network members and attempt to reach an agreement
7 Conduct a review of the focal person's current social network.
8 Make a decision about who to invite and how to approach them
9 Communicate that anyone from the network can continue to attend all treatment sessions, even if other members decide to drop out including the network member
10 End session by giving positive feedback.

PHASE 2: CORE TOPICS

Communication

Working unilaterally with the focal person to involve the network

1 Review inter-session change
2 Explore who might constitute a potential network member
3 Explore the communication skills necessary, to invite them to the meeting
4 Explore one or more of the following as appropriate:
   ⊙ re-establishing contact by telephone
   ⊙ composing a letter to a potential network member
   ⊙ starting conversations
   ⊙ receiving criticism
   ⊙ feeling talk and listening skills
5 End session by giving positive feedback.

Working with the network

1 Welcome new network members and explain their role as per the criteria for Phase 1
2 Review inter-session change
3 Explain the importance of effective communication
4 Explore ways in which the network members can communicate effectively to support the focal person's drinking goals
5 End session by giving positive feedback.

Coping

Working unilaterally with the focal person to involve the network

1 Review inter-session change
2 Discuss the concept of coping and the different ways in which people cope
3 Explore the focal client's understanding of the interactions between themselves and those around them
4 Use the network diagram to explore the ways in which potential network members are coping
5 Discuss how things can be changed in order to engage potential network members
6 If the focal person is isolated, discuss generally the ways of coping and ways they can help alter things
7 End session by giving positive feedback.

Working with the network

1 Welcome new network members and explain their role as per the criteria for Phase 1
2 Review inter-session change
3 Discuss the concept of coping and the different ways in which people cope
4 Discuss the advantages and disadvantages of current and past ways of coping with the focal person's drinking
5 Agree a strategy or policy for helping the focal person's efforts to change
6 End session by giving positive feedback.

Working unilaterally with the network

1 Welcome new network members and explain their role as per the criteria for Phase 1
2 Review inter-session change
3 Explore different ways of coping and the associated advantages and disadvantages
4 Discuss the impact of these strategies upon re-engaging the focal person
5 End session by giving positive feedback.

Coping with relapse

1 Review inter-session change
2 Discuss the concept of coping and the different ways in which people cope
3 Explore how network members are attempting to understand their coping responses to relapse
4 Attempt to reframe relapse as an opportunity for progress rather than as failure
5 End session by giving positive feedback.

Enhancing social support

Unilateral work with the focal person to involve the network

1 Review inter-session change
2 Talk about and identify who is and who is not supportive, and match them to different categories
3 Discuss background material about social support
4 Discuss different types of support
5 Discuss the factors to be considered when developing a social network
6 Use the network map to explore the types and quality of supports that are available
7 End session by giving positive feedback.

Working with the network

1 Welcome new network members and explain their role as per the criteria for Phase 1
2 Review inter-session change

3 Talk about and identify who is and who is not supportive, and match them to different categories
4 Discuss different types of support
5 Discuss the factors to be considered when developing a social network
6 End session by giving positive feedback.

Enhancing support for network members

1 Discuss some of the sources for support failure and how to tackle possible problems
2 Discuss and consider the support needs of network members
3 Identify potential sources of support
4 End session by giving positive feedback.

Network based relapse management

Unilateral work with the focal person to involve the network

1 Review inter-session change
2 Encourage the focal person to think about ways of using the network to support their attempts to avoid lapse or relapse
3 Describe and discuss the concepts and ideas related to relapse and relapse management
4 Devise a strategy that reduces the fear of failure and which may then prevent relapse
5 Identify high risk situations
6 Develop a relapse management plan that involves other people
7 Consider contacts with other agencies such as self-help groups or day centres
8 End session by giving positive feedback.

Working with the network

1 Welcome new network members and explain their role as per the criteria for Phase 1
2 Review inter-session change
3 Describe and discuss the concepts and ideas related to relapse and relapse management
4 Devise a strategy that reduces the fear of failure and which may then prevent relapse
5 Identify high risk situations
6 Agree a policy to be adopted by all members toward risky situations and relapse
7 Develop a plan allocating tasks to all those present
8 End session by giving positive feedback.

PHASE 3: FINAL MEETING

Planning for the future and termination

1 Review inter-session change
2 Discuss how to prepare and plan for the future in dealing with crises that may occur

3 Review previous sessions and encourage the focal person and/or the network members to continue working in the future
4 Encourage the focal person and the network members to see themselves as jointly responsible for ongoing success
5 End session by giving positive feedback.

ELECTIVE TOPICS

Basic information about alcohol

Working unilaterally with the focal person to involve the network

1 Review inter-session change
2 Discuss information set out as an appendix to the manual, especially that which is important to the focal person
3 Explore the understanding of each potential network member as it is perceived by the focal person
4 Explore options for correcting misconceptions by potential network members particularly if they are seen to interfere with network participation
5 End session by giving positive feedback.

Working with the network

1 Review inter-session change
2 Check out with the network members their knowledge and provide any information as appropriate
3 Focus the discussion on attempting to define the extent of the problem and arrive at a view which is shared
4 Discuss how the problem affects everyone present and use this as an opportunity to build toward support and change
5 End session by giving positive feedback.

Increasing pleasant and joint activities

1 Review inter-session change
2 Identify pleasant activities that are relevant to each individual
3 Develop a plan for introducing activities
4 Explore possible strategies to increase activities
5 Consider ways of coping with problems that may arise and that may lead to activities being abandoned
6 Use some of the chosen activities to set homework tasks to be reviewed at the next meeting
7 End session by giving positive feedback

Employment

Working unilaterally with the focal person

1 Review inter-session change
2 Discuss the different tasks involved and help the focal person develop a plan of action
3 Assist the focal person in identifying agencies and how to contact them
4 Set homework to achieve some of the tasks
5 End session by giving positive feedback.

Working with the network

1 Review inter-session change
2 Discuss the different stages and tasks involved
3 Encourage everyone to think about a job seeking plan to support the focal person
4 Facilitate a process whereby the whole network becomes actively involved
5 End session by giving positive feedback.

Active development of positive supports

1 Review inter-session change
2 Help the focal person to initiate a link to a resource who can become a source of positive support
3 Review who in the past has been supportive and in which way
4 Identify the most realistic places where new contacts could be made and introduce the concept of meeting new people
5 As appropriate, use problem-solving techniques to develop strategies to deal with potential problems
6 As appropriate, consider the possibility of the focal person making a telephone call during the meeting and offer practice beforehand
7 As appropriate, consider organising the next meeting to accompany the focal person to the point of making contact with an organisation
8 Set up a homework task that involves some level of achievement
9 End session by giving positive feedback.

Minimising support for problem drinking

1 Review inter-session change
2 Help the focal person to identify where the support for problem drinking is coming from
3 Review who in the past has been supportive of problem drinking

4 Help the focal person to identify people who may pose a problem in terms of risk of relapse
5 Discuss advantages and disadvantages of contact with people who encourage continued drinking
6 Consider options for minimising contact
7 Agree a plan of action
8 End session by giving positive feedback.

The independent rating of the delivery of treatment was based on a separate validated scale which rates the amount and quality of the delivery and its distinctiveness from Motivational Enhancement Therapy (Tober et al. 2008).

COMMON QUESTIONS AND ISSUES RAISED BY THERAPISTS LEARNING TO DELIVER SBNT

In our experience during training and supervision of SBNT we have come across a number of questions posed to us by therapists.

I manage to get significant others to attend once or twice but I find it difficult to keep them engaged in the sessions

It is important to make clear the purpose of the involvement of significant others as part of SBNT sessions. Sometimes, therapists, particularly when they start using the intervention, are able to invite network members initially and are successful in getting them to attend a session. *If the purpose of the network member's attendance is not made clear, however, the likely result is that the network member will start doubting whether he/she can make any contribution to the progress of the focal person and either stop coming or start questioning whether it is useful for him/her to be involved at all.* Network members' involvement, however, is central to the success of the treatment and as such is important. In our experience, we have found that sometimes, therapists assume that network members understand the purpose of their involvement and therefore this is not fully discussed. In reality, they need guidance from the therapist, who operates as a team leader, as to what their role and contribution to the treatment process can be. As a therapist you should always ask yourself at the end of a session during which you engaged a network member whether you have clearly described the purpose of his/her involvement. It may be useful to recap at the end of a session by saying something like:

As we have discussed, the way in which this treatment works is by enhancing or increasing the positive support for change that people have while they are attempting the difficult task of changing their drinking and to try to ensure that this support remains in place for the future. In order to achieve this we need to work directly with all those people who are prepared to offer support and so your attendance at the meetings is extremely important and useful. We are a team with a clear task: to actively support the focal person's attempts to change his/her drinking by identifying things that we can do both over the next few weeks and also in the future.

Encourage network members to ask questions and clarify any doubts they may have about their attendance. Remember that for someone who has never been involved in any form of alcohol treatment, the experience of being in a room trying to support a close relative or friend with a drinking problem may be unusual. *Your task as a therapist and therefore a team leader is to make sure that network members feel they have something positive to offer and therefore are willing to come back to the subsequent sessions.*

I find that sometimes I end up talking mainly to the focal person. It feels like I am doing one-to-one treatments in the presence of other people

Part of the task in SBNT is to make sure that everyone is involved in some way in the change process. In certain situations you may find that because of the characteristics of the people involved, one member of the group, sometimes the focal person, sometimes a network member, monopolises the discussion and after a short while you end up feeling that you are interacting with only one person in a room where other people are present. It is important to try to avoid this situation as it may lead to drop out either by the focal person or network members who do not feel involved. *One way to avoid this situation is to make sure that you ask everyone present to contribute to the discussion at regular intervals.* Make sure you acknowledge any statement made by someone however brief and remember that the essence of the approach is that network members will be able to help the focal person now and in the future. Part of your role is therefore to lay the foundations for this to occur by creating a process whereby everyone is involved and feels part of a team. Ask questions such as 'What did you think of that?' 'Have you experienced this situation?' 'Can you think of examples of this?' 'It must be difficult for everyone when that happens, what do you think?'

At times, I find myself talking too much. It feels more like teaching than leading or facilitating

It is not uncommon to fall into the trap of providing too much information, without creating the opportunity for the group to discuss the material and relate it to their experience. This is also likely to happen when the group is uncertain of the process or people are quiet. *One rule that can be helpful in order to avoid this is never to introduce more than one concept at a time without discussing it with the group and seeking examples from those present as to how this concept relates to their experience.* Always when you introduce a concept you could ask those present to think about ways in which they experienced this in the past. This will also help you to check that everyone has understood the information. For example if you are talking about coping, when you introduce a coping style (e.g. tolerance) you could ask the group to think of examples from their own experience of tolerant coping before you move on to introduce a second coping style. In this way you will be alternating the introduction of new material with discussion and engagement of those present in the session. You will also guarantee that everyone understands the theory in a way that makes it relevant to their own experience.

SBNT is different when you do not have a network

SBNT may look and indeed feel different when you do not have a network. The philosophy however can be applied whether you have managed to engage a network or not. Your ultimate aim is the same, namely to maximise the positive support for change that someone attempting to change his/her drinking has. Sometimes you can start this process with network members in the room but on other occasions you may be able to initiate that process successfully for a client, yet you may not have managed to engage anyone in the treatment sessions. Refer to the diagram earlier on the manual describing the three possible strands of SBNT. It is crucial in these cases to focus on becoming an 'active agent' and look for possible ways of helping the focal client to build positive support.

I can understand the philosophy of **SBNT** even when you are only working with the focal person but sometimes I find myself stuck, repeatedly going over the same ground and trying to convince the focal person to invite a network member sometimes even detecting some resistance

This is a good sign that new strategies need to be tried and more often than not these strategies will involve being 'active agent'. Be prepared to meet the focal person at home for the next session if that is going to maximise the chances of engaging a partner or other family member. If you find yourself in a discussion where you are trying to convince the focal person and he/she comes up with barriers, you could suggest that you could spend the rest of the time available going to meet the network member, or talking to the network member on the telephone, or composing a letter.

As a rule, do not allow yourself to spend too long debating the difficulties in engaging a network member. Try to do something positive to help the focal person to achieve the task rather than getting drawn into his/her own difficulties. Remember that the emphasis is on doing rather than talking.

Sometimes I feel as if I am in the middle of a battleground and the whole meeting seems to drift away from my control

In SBNT this is a clear sign that something has gone wrong and this can result from a number of different problems.

The wrong network members

Sometimes in discussion with the focal person you may have identified a network member and managed to engage this person in the sessions. You may later find that the network member is using the session to vent his/her anger at the focal person in a way that does not allow you to meet the aims of SBNT. A father may be extremely angry with his son, a wife with her husband. *These are normal feelings and understandable but they need to be left aside during SBNT so that the focus is on positive support not criticism or 'confrontation'.* It is easier to anticipate these situations and avoid them rather than deal with them once you are in a session. Take care during the first session to spend enough time exploring with the focal person whether a potential network member is going to be helpful and supportive in the sessions. Remember that your main criterion for choosing network members is that they will support the focal person. If criticism surfaces during the session make sure that you restate clearly and as often as required the purpose of meeting 'to increase positive support for change'. Try to stop negative interactions as soon as they emerge, do not let the criticism go on for any length of time, once you identify this situation, deal with it promptly. You could allow five minutes of 'gripe time' but then the emphasis has to be on solutions.

The wrong focus

It is not uncommon, particularly when feelings are high, to lose the focus of the session and for negative interactions to emerge quickly. Promptly try to bring the focus back to the notion of positive support. State that you understand how people are feeling and how common it is for alcohol problems to give rise to these feelings but how important it is to develop positive support if the aim of maximising the chances of success is to be achieved. If possible, try to work with those network members that are positive and use them as models for other members.

Sometimes it feels as if I am conducting couples therapy. Is this useful for SBNT?

SBNT is different from both marital and family therapies. Some of the key distinctions are outlined in the manual. Sometimes, when you are working with a couple and particularly if there is a certain degree of conflict in the relationship, you may find yourself trying to explore the relationship difficulties in the session. This is *not* the focus of SBNT and therefore this type of work should not be conducted as part of the treatment. *The focus is very clear and specific: 'to elicit positive support for change'. Problems can be explored only if they interfere with the provision of positive support but any significant relationship problems cannot be dealt with in this treatment.* If the relationship problems are severe and interfere with the provision of positive support, you may need to look for alternative forms of help that focus on the relationship problem.

APPENDICES

Handouts and prompt sheets

Drink Diary: For week commencing . . . .

	Name of the drink	Time of day	How much	Number of units	Where and with whom	Cost
Monday						
Tuesday						
Wednesday						
Thursday						
Friday						
Saturday						
Sunday						
				Total		Total

From *Social Behaviour and Network Therapy for Alcohol Problems* by Copello et al. published by Routledge

Information about alcohol and its effects

Alcohol and health

Alcohol is widely available in the western world. People enjoy drinking alcohol for a variety of reasons. Alcohol is used in celebrations such as birthdays and special occasions. Sometimes we drink to make ourselves feel confident or more relaxed. A small amount of alcohol can do little harm and be enjoyable.

How much is it safe to drink

People have different views as to how much it is safe to drink. The most reliable way of knowing whether your drinking is safe is to establish how much alcohol is in your drink. The easiest way to establish the amount of alcohol in a drink is to calculate how many units the drink contains. One unit in the UK contains approximately 8 grams of pure alcohol. The drinks below, for example, have the same level of alcohol content and represent one unit of alcohol:

1 unit = half pint (284ml) of ordinary strength beer, lager or cider
1 unit = one small glass of wine (125ml)
1 unit = one single measure (25ml) of spirits
1 unit = one small glass (50ml) of sherry, martini, port

This description gives you a rough guide to the unit equivalent of common drinks. Beverage alcohol content varies: for example, extra strong beer may contain three times the amount of alcohol contained in ordinary beer.

How much do I drink?

The current advice for safe drinking is that men should not regularly drink more than three to four units on a drinking day and women not

From *Social Behaviour and Network Therapy for Alcohol Problems* by Copello et al. published by Routledge

more than two to three. This is based on the recommendation that consistently drinking four or more units for men and three or more units for women carries the risk of developing health problems over time. It is also emphasised that drinking more than twenty-one units per week for men and more than fourteen units per week for women may increase the risk of harm to health.

If you want to calculate the number of units that you are drinking, you can do so by adding up the drinks you have had over the past few days. Alternatively, there are websites where you can calculate how many units you have consumed (you can do this for example at www.drinkaware. co.uk or www.downyourdrink.org.uk).

What happens to the alcohol I drink?

The alcohol you drink is absorbed in the blood and is later disposed of either through urine or sweat or processed by the liver. The body eliminates approximately one unit of alcohol per hour. The effects of alcohol depend on the amount present in your blood. While one or two drinks may help you feel more relaxed, as you continue to consume alcohol your behaviour may become more problematic. Your decisions may be affected, you might experience loss of inhibition and self-control. Your reaction time may be slowed down, making it more likely to have an accident. If you continue to drink you may lose consciousness and even collapse and die.

Tolerance

When you consume alcohol regularly over a period of time, you may find that you need to consume more alcohol in order to achieve the same effect. This suggests that you may have developed some tolerance to alcohol. Tolerance means that because you have been using alcohol heavily, the effect that it has on you is reduced. You therefore need more of the alcohol in order to have the same experience. In this respect, alcohol is no different to any other drug.

The importance of recognising tolerance is that it is the first step in physical addiction and the development of withdrawal symptoms.

As tolerance develops, you will need to consume an increasing amount of alcohol and may begin to experience withdrawal symptoms when you stop drinking. Withdrawal symptoms include shakes, sweating, feeling

From *Social Behaviour and Network Therapy for Alcohol Problems* by Copello et al. published by Routledge

depressed after stopping or very frightened. In extreme cases you may have fits or see things that are not there. This is happening because your body has become used to functioning with a certain amount of alcohol and when this amount is reduced, your body lets you know through these symptoms. These symptoms can be unpleasant and are usually made worse as a result of the anxiety that people experience as well as their own expectations that the symptoms will be very unpleasant. This creates a vicious circle. Often the way in which the sufferer tries to deal with the problem is by consuming more alcohol, which makes the cycle difficult to break.

Effects of heavy drinking

Heavy drinking over time can result in a range of problems in the physiological, mental and emotional state of the person who is drinking. It results in disruption of a number of responses to the individual's immediate environment. These responses can in turn affect the physical, emotional and social well-being of those close to the person with the drinking problem.

Physically, heavy alcohol consumption can result in damage to organs including the liver and stomach and increase the risk of heart disease and cancer.

Psychologically, a number of changes can occur that will affect not only the drinker but also those close to him or her. Some of the most common experiences are increased risk of violence, depressed mood, the person becoming unreliable, financial hardship and disruption to family routines.

It is possible that many of the things outlined here may not have happened to you. However, it may be that you can relate to most of these descriptions when you consider your past experiences.

On the more positive side, one thing to remember is that even though it is difficult, most people with a drinking problem are able to change even if it takes them several attempts. The amount of support available from those close to the person with the drinking problem and the ways in which they respond will be important.

Impact on others

As someone close to the person with the drinking problem, you may have experienced a roller-coaster of emotions. Early on, you may have

From *Social Behaviour and Network Therapy for Alcohol Problems* by Copello et al. published by Routledge

wondered whether he or she had a problem and if so, how serious it was. You may also have asked yourself if there was anything that you were doing wrong to make the problem worse. In fact, these problems are very common and the experiences you may have had are usually the result of the impact of the drinking problem upon those who are close to the focal drinker. Trying to understand the problem and think about the ways in which you can support your close family member and they can support you will be helpful in the process.

From *Social Behaviour and Network Therapy for Alcohol Problems* by Copello et al. published by Routledge

Communication and the network

Positive communication is important to reduce conflict and division between the social network. Positive communication should result in the focal client and the network working together more constructively and in a unified manner.

When someone develops a problem with alcohol, that person and the people around them will often become stressed. One of the factors that contributes to stress is poor communication.

Possible session tasks

Ask those present:

⊙ Can you give an example of poor communication?
⊙ What were the consequences?
⊙ What could you have done to communicate more effectively?
⊙ What will you do in the future?

Here are some tips to help you . . .

Good communication skills

⊙ Present one issue at a time.
⊙ Define the issue clearly and specifically.
⊙ Speak in a way that is positive and avoids blaming the other person or people.
⊙ Accept partial responsibility for the situation and don't see the other person as being totally at fault.
⊙ Make an offer to help in the situation you are talking about.
⊙ Practice saying what you think without blaming or criticising others.

From *Social Behaviour and Network Therapy for Alcohol Problems* by Copello et al. published by Routledge

How to approach an important person

Sometimes we need to think about approaching new people to develop or enhance our social support network.

On some occasions a relationship may have become difficult or problematic because of our past drinking.

We may want to approach someone we do not know in order to develop a friendship and increase our support network.

Think of *who* you may want to approach.
Decide *what* you would like to say.

Think about difficulties or barriers (e.g. I am not confident starting a conversation; I need to talk to her after all these months and I would not know what to say).

Talk to your therapist or counsellor. You may be able to practise what to say and how to say it. Others have found this very helpful in the past.

You can also ask for help from other friends already in your network.

Practise skills covered under 'receiving criticism and 'talking about feelings and listening skills'.

From *Social Behaviour and Network Therapy for Alcohol Problems* by Copello et al. published by Routledge

Critical statements are highly likely to occur when alcohol use has strained relationships with people close to us. Conflict with others can close off access to positive support and so it is important to learn effective ways of responding to criticism.

Strategies for dealing with criticism

Don't counterattack with further criticism. This will only make the argument worse and decrease the chance of effective communication.

Instead

⊙ It can be effective to begin by acknowledging the other person's feelings and try to find something in their criticism that you can agree with.

'I know that things have been difficult between us and that part of this is related to my drinking.'

⊙ Ask for more information about the criticism so that you are clearer about what the other person means.

'I am not clear why you feel this way and it would be helpful to me to know more.'

⊙ Propose a workable solution. This is something you agree to change to meet the criticism.

'I really value our relationship and I would like to find a compromise. Perhaps you could help me to change this behaviour . . .'

⊙ Reject unwarranted criticism. Sometimes criticism is unjustified. Reject criticism politely but firmly.

'I understand that you are angry but I don't think it is fair to say that. I am making an effort to change by (e.g. attending treatment) and I would really appreciate your support with this.'

From *Social Behaviour and Network Therapy for Alcohol Problems* by Copello et al. published by Routledge

Talking about feelings

Many people have difficulty expressing their feelings and/or listening to the feelings of others. These communication skills can be improved to help you communicate with your network more effectively.

- It's fine to talk about your feelings.
- It is important to share both positive and negative feelings.
- The goal is *not* to share all your deepest feelings with everybody. Instead *appropriate self-disclosure* is a better guide to follow.

From *Social Behaviour and Network Therapy for Alcohol Problems* by Copello et al. published by Routledge

A
P
P
E
N
D
I
X | 7

Coping

The network members' responses to the alcohol problem are known as 'coping'.

When faced with an alcohol problem, network members will attempt to respond to the situation. This involves using different coping strategies. The difficulty is that the strategies tend to be based on partial information and on the network members' attitudes and feelings. It is therefore helpful for network members to work with the focal person better to understand the situation so that they can respond more effectively.

Different ways of coping lead to different results, both for network members and the focal alcohol user. Research has identified that people fit into three broad categories of coping, which are *engaged*, *tolerant* and *withdrawal*.

Task: explore how you respond to others and how they react to you

Familiarise yourself with the common types of coping and identify what type or types of coping you use. They are:

- *Engaged*: attempts to change alcohol use (e.g. watch him or her all the time; plead with him or her; pour the alcohol down the sink). This may help the person who is using this coping style to feel in control but it is also very stressful.
- *Tolerant*: attempts to protect the alcohol user from the negative consequences of the alcohol use (e.g. giving the focal client money for drink; seeing them drink in your presence). This may avoid conflict but can also make the person feel used and taken advantage of.
- *Withdrawal*: attempts to put distance between the network member and the focal client (e.g. spending less time with the focal client; going away for periods of time). It may make the network member feel that they are rejecting the focal drinker.

Think of the pros and cons of your coping style and the alternative ways of coping.

After exploring the different ways you can respond, try to identify what might be the most helpful way of responding to each other in particular situations that might arise in the future.

From *Social Behaviour and Network Therapy for Alcohol Problems* by Copello et al. published by Routledge

Enhancing social support

Research has shown that a positive support network helps people to feel more confident in managing their lives and cope with their problems.

Positive support

A positive network member is simply someone who is focused on helping you to overcome your alcohol problem.

A neutral network member is someone who is neither supportive nor non-supportive. This network member has potential to be more supportive.

An unhelpful network member is a person who is neither supportive nor helpful. They could be individuals who would hinder your efforts to overcome your drinking problem and you need to reduce contact with them.

Task: Can you identify who the positive, neutral and unhelpful network members are in your social support?

Types of support

Social support can take on many forms. Some types of support that research has found to be important to our well-being include help with solving problems, moral support, practical support and help with information or dealing with emergencies.

Task: Can you identify what type of support each member in your network gives you?

Developing your social network

It might be that not all support needs are being met. You might need to work on how you can work with your network to meet your needs. Maybe you need to take another look at who is out there for you.

From *Social Behaviour and Network Therapy for Alcohol Problems* by Copello et al. published by Routledge

Tasks: Looking at your network

- ⊙ Is there anyone who could meet your needs better?
- ⊙ Can you add more supporters to your network to fulfill the different types of support that you need?
- ⊙ How do you support others?

From *Social Behaviour and Network Therapy for Alcohol Problems* by Copello et al. published by Routledge

APPENDIX 9

Relapse prevention

Relapse prevention is an important topic because it aims to put in place methods for the focal person and network member to work together to identify times when a person might be at risk of falling back into problem drinking.

Network members may find this a difficult notion to accept but it is a common pattern for clients to have a lapse or sometimes a full relapse.

A *lapse* is simply a short-lived and usually isolated return to problem drinking. The focal client is usually able to continue back quickly towards his/her treatment goal.

A *relapse* is where the client returns to the level of drinking that he/she had prior to treatment. The most common reason for this is that a client may not be ready to change or has not set goals that are fully realistic and achievable.

Within SBNT we try to avoid lapses and relapses by ensuring that we spend time setting a very realistic goal in the first session. We can also use this relapse management session to look at situations in which the focal client is most vulnerable to lapsing and how the network can help him/her to avoid these situations or stressors.

Task: it is useful to think of situations you might have been in previously:

⊙ Identify high risk situations and stressors for alcohol use that might occur in the future (when, where, with whom).
⊙ Identify thoughts and feelings that occur in the events preceding these situations.
⊙ Agree an overall policy (people to call, help groups) that can be adopted to avoid high risk situations in future.

From *Social Behaviour and Network Therapy for Alcohol Problems* by Copello et al. published by Routledge

10

Increasing pleasant and joint activities

When someone develops an alcohol problem, this may result in a reduction in pleasurable activities for everyone. Below are some reasons why increasing pleasant activities can be helpful:

⦿ Increases positive feelings and mutual support
⦿ Provides alternative activities to problem drinking
⦿ Leads to meeting new people who are positive
⦿ Helps to reduce the amount of time spend with more negative influences.

SBNT is about getting positive support for change. Pleasant activities increase the chances of finding positive support in a person's life and reduce the chances of being around a more negative network that could trigger problematic drinking.

This session is very practical and involves a series of tasks.

Task 1: Can you brainstorm all of the activities you enjoy?

⦿ What have you done in the past?
⦿ What do your network members do?
⦿ What activities would you like to do?

Task 2: Discuss these activities with the therapist

⦿ Are there any barriers to achieving these activities?
⦿ What are the pros and cons?

Task 3: Make a plan of how you will do this activity

⦿ What steps do you need to take in order to be doing this activity?
⦿ Can anyone help you with this?
⦿ Can you be really specific and state dates and times?

From *Social Behaviour and Network Therapy for Alcohol Problems* by Copello et al. published by Routledge

References

Abbott, P.J., Weller, S.B., Delaney, H.D. and Moore, B.A. (1998). Community reinforcement approach in the treatment of opiate addicts. *American Journal of Drug and Alcohol Abuse*, 24: 17–30.

Adams, P.J. (2008). *Fragmented Intimacy: Addiction in a Social World*. Auckland, NZ: Springer.

Azrin, N. (1976). Improvements in the community reinforcement approach to alcoholism. *Behaviour Research and Therapy*, 14: 339–348.

Azrin, N., Sisson, R., Meyers, R. and Godley, M. (1982). Alcoholism treatment by disulfiram and community reinforcement. *Journal of Behaviour Therapy and Experimental Psychiatry*, 13: 105–112.

Barber, J.G. and Crisp, B.R. (1995). The 'pressures to change' approach to working with the partners of heavy drinkers. *Addiction*, 90: 268–276.

Beattie, M.C., Longabaugh, R., Elliot, G., Stout, R.L., Fava, J. and Noel, N.E. (1993). The effect of social environment on alcohol involvement and subjective well-being prior to alcoholism treatment. *Journal of Studies on Alcohol*, 54: 283–296.

Chaney, E., O'Leary, M. and Marlatt, G. (1978). Skill training with alcoholics. *Journal of Consulting and Clinical Psychology*, 46: 1092–1104.

Copello, A., Moore, A. and Orford, J. (1997). *Network Support Therapy: Mobilising a Positive Network to Support a Change in Drinking*. Birmingham: University of Birmingham.

Copello, A., Templeton, L., Krishnan, M., Orford, J. and Velleman, R. (2000a). A treatment package to improve primary care services for relatives of people with alcohol and drug problems. *Addiction Research*, 8: 471–484.

Copello, A., Orford, J., Velleman, R., Templeton, L. and Krishnan, M. (2000b). Methods for reducing alcohol and drug related family harm in non-specialist settings. *Journal of Mental Health*, 9: 329–343.

Copello, A., Orford, J., Hodgson, R., Tober, G. and Barrett, C. on behalf of the UKATT Research Team (2002). Social Behaviour and Network Therapy: basic principles and early experiences. *Addictive Behaviors*, 27: 345–366.

Copello, A., Velleman, R. and Templeton, L. (2005). Family interventions in the treatment of alcohol and drug problems. *Drug and Alcohol Review*, 24: 369–385.

Copello, A., Templeton, L. and Velleman, R. (2006a). Family intervention for drug and alcohol misuse: is there a best practice? *Current Opinion in Psychiatry*, 19: 271–276.

Copello, A., Williamson, E., Orford, J. and Day, E. (2006b). Implementing and evaluating Social Behaviour and Network Therapy in drug treatment practice in the UK: a feasibility study. *Addictive Behaviors*, 31: 802–810.

Ellis, J. (1998). *A Quasi Experimental Trial of Network Support Therapy for Alcohol Problems*. Unpublished Clin PsyD thesis, University of Birmingham.

Finney, J. and Monahan, S. (1996). The cost-effectiveness of treatment for alcoholism: a second approximation. *Journal of Studies on Alcohol*, 57: 229–243.

Galanter, M. (1993a). *Network Therapy for Alcohol and Drug Abuse: A New Approach in Practice*. New York: Basic Books.

Galanter, M. (1993b). Network therapy for substance abuse: a clinical trial. *Psychotherapy*, 30: 251–258.

Galvani, S. (2007). Safety in numbers? Tackling domestic abuse in couples and network therapies. *Drug and Alcohol Review*, 26: 175–181.

Goldfried, M. and D'Zurilla, T. (1969). A behaviour-analytic model for assessing competence. In: C. Spielberger (ed.) *Current Topics in Clinical and Community Psychology*. New York: Academic Press.

Gruber, K., Chutuape, M. and Stitzer, M. (2000). Reinforcement-based intensive outpatient treatment for inner city opiate abusers: a short term evaluation. *Drug and Alcohol Dependence*, 57 (3): 211–223.

Hasin, D.S. (1994). Treatment/self-help for alcohol-related problems: relationship to social pressure and alcohol dependence. *Journal of Studies on Alcohol*, 55: 660–666.

Higgins, S.T., Sigmon, S.C., Wong, C.J., Heil, S.H., Badger, G.J., Donham, R., Dantona, R.L. and Anthony, S. (1993). Community reinforcement therapy for cocaine-dependent outpaitents. *Archives of General Psychiatry*, 60:, 1043–1052.

Holder, H., Longabaugh, R., Miller, W. and Rubonis, A. (1991). The cost effectiveness of treatment for alcoholism: a first approximation. *Journal of Studies on Alcohol*, 52: 517–540.

Howells, E. and Orford, J. (2006). Coping with a problem drinker: a therapeutic intervention for the partners of problem drinkers, in their own right. *Journal of Substance Use*, 11: 53–71.

Hunt, G. and Azrin, N. (1973). The community reinforcement approach to alcoholism. *Behaviour Research and Therapy*, 11: 91–104.

Kelley, M.L. and Fals-Stewart, B.F. (2002). Couples- versus individual-based therapy for alcohol and drug abuse: effects on children's psychosocial functioning. *Journal of Consulting and Clinical Psychology*, 70: 417–427.

Kellner, R. and Sheffield, B. (1973). A self rating scale of distress. *Psychological Medicine*, 3: 88–100.

Leventhal, H., Meyer, D. and Nerenz, D. (1980). The commonsense representation of illness danger. In: S. Rachman. *Medical Psychology*. Tarytown, NY: Pergamon.

Litt, M.D., Kadden, R.M., Kabela-Cormier, E. and Petry, N. (2007). Changing network support for drinking: initial findings from the network support project. *Journal of Consulting and Clinical Psychology*, 75: 542–555.

Longabaugh, R., Beattie, M., Noel, N., Stout, R. and Malloy, P. (1993). The effect of social investment on treatment outcome. *Journal of Studies on Alcohol*, 54: 465–478.

McCrady, B.S. (2004). To have but one true friend: implications for practice of research on alcohol use disorders and social networks. *Psychology of Addictive Behaviors*, 18: 113–121.

McCrady, B., Noel, N., Abrams, D., Stout, R., Nelson, H. and Hay, W. (1986). Comparative effectiveness of three types of spouse involvement in outpatient behavioral alcoholism treatment. *Journal of Studies on Alcohol*, 47: 459–467.

McCrady, B.S., Stout, R.L., Noel, N.E., Abrams, D.B. and Nelson, H.F. (1990). Comparative effectiveness of three types of spouse involved behavioural alcoholism treatment: outcomes 18 months after treatment. In: R.L. Collins, K.E. Leonard and J.S. Searles (eds.) *Alcohol and the Family: Research and Clinical Perspectives*. Guilford Substance Abuse series. New York: Guilford Press.

McCrady, B.S., Epstein, E.E. and Hirsh, L.S. (1999). Maintaining change after conjoint behavioral alcohol treatment for men: outcomes at six months. *Addiction*, 94: 1381–1396.

Marlatt, A. and Gordon, J. (eds) (1985). *Relapse Prevention: Maintenance Strategies in the Treatment of Addictive Behaviours*. New York: Guilford Press.

Meads, C.M., Ting, S., Dretzke, J. and Bayliss, S. (2007). A systematic review of the clinical and cost-effectiveness of psychological therapy involving family and friends in alcohol misuse or dependence. Report by Department of Public Health and Epidemiology, West Midlands Health Technology Assessment Group, University of Birmingham.

Meyers, R.J. and Smith, J.E. (1995). *Clinical Guide to Alcohol Treatment: The Community Reinforcement Approach*. New York: Plenum.

Meyers, R.J., Dominguez, T.P. and Smith, J.E. (1996). Community reinforcement training with concerned others. In: V.B. Van Hasselt and R.K. Hersen (eds) *Sourcebook of Psychological Treatment Manual for Adult Disorders*. New York: Plenum.

Miller, W. and Mount, K. (2001). A small study of training in motivational interviewing: does one workshop change clinician and client behaviour? *Behavioural and Cognitive Psychotherapy*, 29: 457–471.

Miller, W. and Wilbourne, P. (2002). Mesa Grande: a methodological analysis of clinical trials of treatments for alcohol use disorders. *Addiction*, 97: 265–277.

Miller, W.R., Meyers, R.J. and Tonigan, J.S. (1999). Engaging the unmotivated in treatment for alcohol problems: a comparison of three strategies for intervention through family members. *Journal of Consulting and Clinical Psychology*, 67: 688–697.

Mohr, C.D., Averna, S., Kenny, D.A. and Del Boca, F.K. (2001). 'Getting by (or getting high) with a little help from my friends': an examination of adult alcoholics' friendships. *Journal on Studies of Alcohol*, 62: 637–645.

Molloy, D.J. (1989). Peer intervention: an exploratory study. *Journal of Drug Issues*, 19: 319–336.

Monti, P.M., Kadden, R.M., Rohsenow, D.J., Cooney, N.L. and Abrams, D.B. (2002). *Treating Alcohol Dependence: A Coping Skills Training Guide*, 2nd edn. New York: Guilford Press.

Nowinski, J., Baker, S. and Carroll, K. (1995). *Twelve Step Facilitation Therapy Manual*. Project MATCH monograph series volume 1. Bethesda, MD: National Institute on Alcohol Abuse and Alcoholism.

O'Farrell, T.J. and Fals-Stewart, W. (2006). *Behavioral Couples Therapy for Alcoholism and Drug Abuse*. New York: Guilford Press.

O'Farrell, T.J. and Murphy, C.M. (1995). Marital violence before and after alcoholism treatment. *Journal of Consulting and Clinical Psychology*, 63: 256–262.

O'Farrell, T.J., Cutter, H.S.G. and Floyd, F.J. (1985). Evaluating behavioral marital therapy for male alcoholics: effects of marital adjustment and communication before and after treatment. *Behavior Therapy*, 16: 147–167.

O'Farrell, T.J., Cutter, H.S.G., Choquette, K.A., Floyd, F.J. and Bayog, R.D. (1992). Behavioral marital therapy for male alcoholics: marital and drinking adjustment during the two years after treatment. *Behavior Therapy*, 23: 529–549.

O'Farrell, T.J., Choquette, K.A., Cutter, H.S.G., Brown, E.D. and McCourt, W.F. (1993). Behavioral marital therapy with and without additional couples relapse prevention sessions for alcoholics and their wives. *Journal of Studies on Alcohol*, 54: 652–666.

Orford, J. (1994). Empowering family and friends: a new approach to the prevention of alcohol and drug problems. *Drug and Alcohol Review*, 13: 417–429.

Orford, J. (1998). The coping perspective. In: R. Velleman, A. Copello and J. Maslin (eds) *Living with Drink: Women who Live with Problem Drinkers*. London: Longmans.

Orford, J., Guthrie, S., Nicolls, P., Oppenheimer, E., Egert, S. and Hensman, C. (1975). Self-reported coping behaviour of wives of alcoholics in association with drinking outcome. *Journal of Studies on Alcohol*, 36: 1254–1267.

Orford, J., Rigby, K., Miller, T., Tod, A., Bennett, G. and Velleman, R. (1992). Ways of coping with excessive drug use in the family: a provisional typology based on the accounts of 50 close relatives. *Journal of Community and Applied Social Psychology*, 2: 163–183.

Orford, J., Natera, G., Davies, J., Nava, A., Mora, J., Rigby, K., Bradbury, C., Copello, A. and Velleman, R. (1998a). Stresses and strains for family members living with drinking or drug problems in England and Mexico. *Salud Mental*, 21: 1–13.

Orford, J., Natera G., Davies J., Nava A., Mora J., Rigby K., Bradbury C., Bowie N., Copello A. and Velleman R. (1998b). Tolerate, engage or withdraw: a study of the structure of family coping in England and Mexico. *Addiction*, 93: 1799–1813.

Orford, J., Natera, G., Davies, J., Nava, A., Mora, J., Rigby, K., Bradbury, C., Copello, A. and Velleman, R. (1998c). Social support in coping with alcohol and drug problems at home: findings from Mexican and English families. *Addiction Research*, 6: 395–420.

Orford, J., Natera, G., Copello, A., Atkinson, C., Mora, J., Velleman, R., Crundall, I., Tiburcio, M., Templeton, L. and Walley, G. (2005). *Coping with Alcohol and Drug Problems: The Experiences of Family Members in Three Contrasting Cultures*. London: Brunner-Routledge.

Orford, J., Templeton, L., Copello, A., Velleman, R., Ibanga, A. and Binnie, C. (2009). Increasing the involvement of family members in alcohol and drug treatment services: the results of an action research project in two specialist agencies. *Drugs: Education, Prevention and Policy*.

Project MATCH Research Group. (1997). Matching alcoholism treatment to client heterogeneity: Project MATCH post-treatment drinking outcomes. *Journal of Studies on Alcohol*, 58: 1671–1698.

Sisson, R. and Azrin, N. (1989). The community reinforcement approach. In R. Hester and W. Miller (eds) *Handbook of Alcoholism Treatment Approaches*. New York: Pergamon.

Smith, J.E., Meyers, R.J. and Miller, W.R. (2001). The community reinforcement approach to the treatment of substance use disorders. *American Journal on Addictions*, 10: 51–59.

Stanton, M.D. and Shadish, W.R. (1997). Outcome, attrition, and family – couples treatment for drug abuse: a meta-analysis and review of the controlled, comparative studies. *Psychological Bulletin*, 122: 170–191.

Stout, R.L., McCrady, B.S., Longabough, R., Noel, N.E. and Beattie, M.C. (1987). Marital therapy enhances the long-term effectiveness of alcohol treatment. *Alcohol Clinical Experimental Research*, 11: 213.

Stout, R.L., McCrady, B.S., Longabaugh, R., Noel, N.E. and Beattie, M.C. (1990). Marital therapy helps to maintain the effectiveness of alcohol treatment: replication of an outcome crossover effect. In: R.L. Collins, K.E. Leonard and J.S. Searles (eds) *Alcohol and the Family: Research and Clinical Perspectives*. Guilford Substance Abuse series. New York: Guilford Press.

Thomas, E.J. and Ager, R.D. (1993). Unilateral family therapy. In: T.J. O'Farrell (ed.) *Treating Alcohol Problems: Marital and Family Interventions*. London: Guilford Press.

Tober, G., Godfrey, C., Parrott, S., Copello, A., Farrin, A., Hodgson, R., Kenyon, R., Morton, V., Orford, J., Russell, I. and Slegg, G. on behalf of the UKATT Research Team (2005).

Setting standards for training and competence: the UK Alcohol Treatment Trial. *Alcohol and Alcoholism*, 40: 413–418.

Tober, G., Clyne, W., Finnegan, O., Farrin, A. and Russell, I. in collaboration with the UKATT Research Team (2008). Validation of a scale for rating the delivery of psycho-social treatments for alcohol dependence and misuse: the UKATT Process Rating Scale (PRS). *Alcohol and Alcoholism*, 43: 675–682.

UKATT Research Team (2005a). Effectiveness of treatment for alcohol problems: findings of the randomised United Kingdom Alcohol Treatment Trial (UKATT). *British Medical Journal*, 331: 541–544.

UKATT Research Team (2005b). Cost-effectiveness of treatment for alcohol problems: findings of the randomised United Kingdom Alcohol Treatment Trial (UKATT). *British Medical Journal*, 331: 544–558.

Walitzer, K. and Dermen, K. (2004). Alcohol-focused spouse involvement and behavioural couples therapy: evaluation of enhancements to drinking reduction treatment for male problem drinkers. *Journal of Consulting and Clinical Psychology*, 72: 944–955.

Yates, F.E. (1988). The evaluation of a 'co-operative counselling' alcohol service which uses families and affected others to reach and influence problem drinkers. *British Journal of Addiction*, 83: 1309–1319.

Index

Note: References in *italic* refer to case studies, those in **bold** to handouts/prompt sheets.